Take Control of your Confidence

The inside track to unleashing
your potential

To make bulk purchases of this book or to obtain further information about other publications and services from Track Record, please contact:

Marketing Department

Track Record

An imprint of Track Record Coaching Ltd

15 Bury Walk
London
SW3 6QD
UK

Tel: +44(0) 7912 556483

Email: hello@trackrecord.coach

Take Control of your Confidence

The Inside Track to Unleashing your Potential

David Carry, Dr Hannah MacLeod, Katherine Moore
and Dr Scott Gardner

Contents

Foreword

Clare Balding: Writer and Broadcaster

I have always loved reporting on sport because I enjoy seeing people perform under pressure. The human body and mind are extraordinary things and often capable of far more than we expect or predict. I also love the authenticity of sport. You can't pretend or hide or take the day off because you don't feel like it. That is why a book like this, written by those who understand what it takes to succeed in a sporting environment, can teach us so much about our own lives.

This is quite a writing team – Olympic swimmer David Carry, Olympic hockey gold medallist Hannah MacLeod, physiotherapist and sports scientist Katherine Moore and Cycling performance coach Dr Scott Gardner. They have an undisputed and impressive track record. They've experienced success and failure and they are willing to share what they have learned. From real life experience, they talk from the heart about preparation, organisation, discipline, communication, motivation, efficiency of time and energy, ambition, overcoming the fear of failure, the power of good teamwork and the all-important execution of what we have learned. It is thoroughly revealing and instructive.

Athletes have to be honest about themselves to achieve their potential. They cannot fake training, they cannot lie about times or goals or technique, they cannot short-change themselves on recovery or stint on preparation. It will all show in the cold, clear glare of the public gaze. Those who have purpose, commitment and vision will respect the process that needs to be followed to give themselves a chance of success. The outcome may depend on their ability to seize that chance but if there are no foundations, the whole edifice will crumble.

The history of sport is full of individuals achieving the impossible – Eliud Kipchoge running a marathon in under two hours, Ben Stokes scoring 135 not out to win the Test match at Headingley against Australia to keep the Ashes alive, Simone Biles winning more world championship medals in gymnastics than her age (24 medals at the age of 22). We may not reach such heights of sporting excellence, but this is a book for mere mortals to find a way towards our own 'win'.

Reading this exceptional guide has helped me find a clarity of thought about how I go about daily life, what I want to achieve and what I need to do to get there. It has also made me redefine my values. I have always been clear about what I do and don't want to do but giving myself a framework of written values has really helped me explain to others why I make the choices I do. I may have been guilty in the past of 'delusional optimism' as defined in Chapter 5, when I have just hoped something into existence without preparing properly, but I know from experience that doing your homework in a broadcast environment really does pay dividends. I may not need all the facts at the same time and I may even get through a programme without needing a tenth of them but at some point, without warning, I know that I will have to 'fill' for an unspecified length of time and that's when knowing about the previous Olympics held in London or understanding the history of the Paralympics will come in pretty handy.

I have also learned, as I head towards my seventh Olympic Games, that I have to be physically and mentally fit to maintain my energy and performance levels for 17 consecutive days of long hours and fast thinking. I need healthy food, plenty of sleep and limited alcohol. It's nice to have time out with the team and it helps on screen bonding but it's not a social event - it's a major work commitment and it only comes around once every four years. The party can wait.

The most powerful message of 'Take Control', I think, is that we are not victims of our surroundings or our circumstances. We do make our own choices; we prioritise knowingly, and we should take responsibility for the decisions we make. That doesn't mean blaming ourselves endlessly when things go wrong or feeling guilty because we haven't spent time with the family or we didn't go to the gym when we should have done, but it does mean being honest about what we want from life and spelling out to ourselves how we are going to get there.

I believe in taking control of your own narrative, writing the story as you want it to be told and living up to it - but it's not easy. As a freelance broadcaster and writer, I try to spin a lot of plates in working for different organisations. I have often been guilty, as I am sure is common with many of us, of being a 'busy fool', running round and round in circles trying to do a bit here and a bit there, keeping everyone happy and exhausting myself in the process. This book has helped me find focus, analyse patterns of behaviour and give myself a clearer structure to help move my life from haphazard chaos to enjoyable but structured variety.

There is a lot of talk these days about 'living your best life'. I always thought that sounded a bit hedonistic and selfish but in reading 'Take Control' I now realise that living your best life is not about playing golf when you fancy it and taking off on holiday all the time, it's about finding focus and meaning. To do that, I, like everyone else, need to be honest about where I am and where I want to get. The first step is reading this book. The next is putting it into action.

Clare Balding
October 2019

Preface

We have had first hand experience through our experiences in elite sport that high levels of confidence lead to high levels of performance, which in turn lead to high levels of success.

We have then taken those experiences and looked to other high performing teams across the world; in business, sport, military and even astronauts to decode what it takes to win.

The unifying factor was psychological, and that psychological factor was confidence. However, the confidence you need to win may not be your current definition of confidence. We wrote this book to share our definition and its components to enable individuals to immediately apply this to their own lives and be in control of their own success.

We are on a 40 year mission to ensure that everybody has the opportunity to be in control of their choices, design their own life and own their own confidence in order to fulfil their potential.

David, Katherine, Hannah and Scott

Introduction

What does it mean to control your confidence?

If you have ever felt you have not been able to give your best performance, never felt you've been able to achieve the results deep down you think you deserve, then you need to read this book.

This book decodes the things you need to be more successful and more fulfilled. Imagine being totally prepared, knowing that your next choice will bring you closer to your desired ambition.

We have had the good fortune to work with, and be surrounded by, some of the world's best athletes and confidence has been an essential companion for each successful person, team or organisation.

This book will focus on you.

We won't tell you to set unrealistic targets, or make you feel guilty about your life to date. We have experienced more than our fair share of disappointments and missed opportunities, and through our failures and our studies we have unlocked the magic formula to success. Except it isn't a formula at all. It is a very simple message: in order to achieve the success you deserve, all you need is confidence. Real, pure, earned, informed confidence. And we know exactly how to help you find your inner confidence and convert it into a win.

Confidence and success often go hand in hand. Think of the purposeful swagger of a newly-elected politician, or the riotous celebrations of a sports team after a huge victory – there is no space for shrinking violets among the world's winners.

But confidence does not come from success – it comes from within. We can only feel confident when we are sure of ourselves and our place in the world. It is a sense of knowing what we stand for, and being true to those values. That confidence is reinforced by our actions and behaviour, and it is eventually rewarded when we realise our unique purpose and achieve win after win.

We have named this book 'Take Control of your Confidence' because used correctly, confidence can propel us forward and help us to achieve our full potential, whether that is in life, in sport or in business. However, confidence alone is not enough. There must be a structure in place for us to follow – a roadmap to success.

We know this because we have lived it. The Track Record team is made up of Olympic medalists, sports science and medicine practitioners and storied coaches, we have all harnessed our own confidence to achieve a series of milestones and wins. We have done this by looking inward, and remaining focused so that we can deliver our best possible performance at the moment of execution.

What is the win?
We don't like to use the word goal, if possible. A goal represents a tangible thing – a one-off, momentary experience that is over as soon as it has begun. Instead, we use the word 'win'. A win is enduring because it is earned through hard work and dedication. An Olympic champion will always be an Olympic champion – just as a doctor is always a doctor, a mother is always a mother, and a company's founder is always that company's founder. Furthermore, each one of us can experience multiple

wins throughout our lives at any one time. David Carry is not 'just' an Olympic athlete, he is also a husband, a father, an ambassador and a businessman.

This book can be used again and again to help you to achieve any number of different wins in your life. It's just a matter of taking it choice-by-choice.

How to use this book

We have designed this book to be easy to use, and even easier to re-use. Each chapter represents a choice that we must make in order to give ourselves the greatest chance of achieving our win. We begin by setting our foundations, and then we drill down into each one of our values and aspirations to make sure that we are always acting in a way that is true to ourselves.

Then we interrogate our plans by time-travelling to our win, to expose any gaps in our plan and to gain clarity on it.

We then move on to explore the critical elements which are required in order to achieve any type of win. Each critical element must be fulfilled before we can move on to the next stage. This is a detailed process that involves plenty of lists and may lead to some substantial lifestyle changes. However, if we can get through this part of the process, we will be well on our way the win.

Once we understand what needs to be done and what needs to be avoided, we can focus on planning, and then on the execution of the win itself. Finally, we will discover how to extend our win through learning, and by creating a legacy for ourselves – and others – to follow.

There are eight distinct choices that we all must make on our way to the win. Each of these choices is equally important, and each is backed up by our own anecdotes and both academic and scientific research. Every one of us at Track Record has lived this process, and we have witnessed great things in our clients' lives when they have followed these eight choices as well.

On your first read, we recommend starting at the beginning and working through to the end – pausing at those chapters where a little more time is required.

After that, the book can be used to help guide you on your way to any future wins. Refer to chapter seven when you are struggling to maintain your mindset, or to chapter three when you need to be reminded of your foundations.

This book is intended to be a map to success, and we encourage you to interact with it as much as possible, filling out the tables in the 'How to Apply' sections, and considering every question which is asked along the way. The more you do this, the more personal this journey will become, and the more valuable this book will be in your future.

Who is this book for?
This is a book for anyone who has every felt frustrated at their lack of confidence and felt that they could do better or aim higher than they have in the past.

It is also a book for us – the athletes and coaches who make up Track Record. This book is the accumulation of our own unique experiences – our failures and our successes and everything in between. It is a reflection of our extensive studies in the field of sports psychology and psychology in general, and the lessons we have drawn from historical and modern day 'winners' as well. We have researched academic papers, referenced scientific studies and quoted renowned thinkers and writers. We have also shared some intimate moments from our own lives, to demonstrate the real-life impact that these studies can have.

By collating all of this into one place, we are creating a playbook for success that each member of Track Record has used. By sharing it with the world, we hope that this book can change lives and help every one of its readers to grow in confidence so that you too can ignite your true potential. And it all starts from deep within.

The Atomic Model

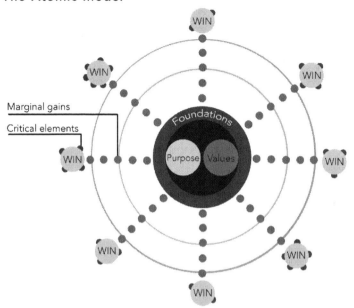

Our Atomic Confidence Model appears in every chapter of this book, because it contains the one essential piece of knowledge that is necessary to success: that success – and the confidence to pursue that success – is inside all of us, at an atomic level.

Within the nucleus lie the proton and neutrons. These can be viewed as purpose (proton), identity (neutrons) and foundations (nucleus). They are at the core of every atom in our bodies, creating our stable core structure.

The electrons are the wins we wish to achieve in our life. They buzz around, come and go but are ultimately attracted to the nucleus. By focusing too much on the electrons at the expense of our nucleus then we will end up with the unfulfilled feeling of chasing the unattainable. But if we have too much of an introspective focus on the nucleus, then nothing will happen.

Achieving a healthy balance between knowing who we are at our core, the ambition we are striving for and being prepared to do what it takes to achieve your ambitious wins is the essence of confidence.

Confidence

Confidence is critical to increasing the probability of success. In fact, confidence has been identified as one of the most important psychological contributors to a positive outcome in sport, in business and in life.

We explore confidence from multiple perspectives: there's the confidence that we have as individuals; and the confidence that we have when we step into a team or organisation.

When we look at confidence from an individual perspective, it is easy to see how a higher performance level becomes more likely when individuals believe in their own abilities to succeed. On an individual level, confidence helps us to walk taller, to make better decisions, and to set ambitious goals that we then strive to reach.

At a team level interdependence is very high, and the confidence of each player in the team's performance is just as important as their own self-confidence. Evidence suggests that teams with a high collective confidence perform at a higher level than teams with a low collective confidence. In fact, team confidence may even be a more powerful force than an individual's strengths, when it comes to giving a successful performance.

Confidence comes from knowing who we are and leaning into our individual and collective strengths. It is a combination of our values, purpose and identity, as well as our ability to interact with the world around us.

This confidence already exists inside of us. It is embedded within the nucleus of our every atom, and it represents our enormous potential. Yet many of us overlook this potential and focus too much on the electrons.

But here's the problem – the behaviour of electrons is notoriously hard to predict. They buzz around constantly, interacting with the outside world and being impacted by all sorts of environmental factors. If we make our decisions based on these electrons, we are leaving a lot up to chance.

By contrast, if we base our decisions from the point of view of the nucleus, we are starting out in a position of control, or stability, where everything stems from our own values and identity. From this stable centre, we can clearly establish our purpose.

The further inside the nucleus we go, the more stable it becomes. The further out we go, the more uncontrollable it gets.

When it comes to setting and achieving goals, we will always be influenced to a certain extent by external factors such as our environment and our resources. But by focusing on the nucleus, we can give ourselves the best chance of success. This is how we build our confidence and lay the foundations for success.

Chapter 1

Discover your purpose
– Why am I here?

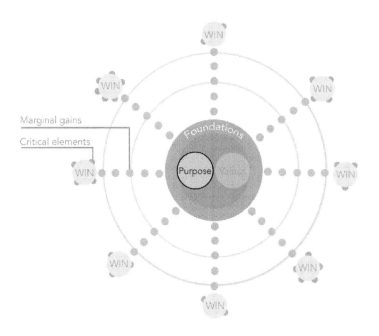

1.1 INTRODUCING PURPOSE

What is your purpose?

We are all here for a unique purpose, but this purpose will not always be obvious. Most of us will have to seek out and identify our purpose, whether that means setting new standards in the sport of our choice, parenting a child, or building a meaningful career.

Although we may not consciously know this, or even acknowledge it, a belief in purpose is the 'why' that lies at the core of each and every one of us, generating our motivation and accelerating our desire to achieve. It is the first step towards success and the foundation for a life of confidence and accomplishment. In the Atomic Model, we have placed purpose right at the heart of the nucleus because it is the starting point for all the work to come. When our sense of purpose is strong, it stabilises our core and helps us to build confidence from the inside out.

A sense of purpose has even been linked with our health and life expectancy. In a paper titled 'Subjective wellbeing, health, and ageing"(1), researchers found that eudemonic wellbeing (purpose and meaning in life) is associated with increased survival. Following a nine-year study, it was revealed that 29·3% of people in the lowest wellbeing quartile died during the average follow-up period of 8·5 years compared with 9·3% of those in the highest quartile. A similar research study by Northwestern University (2) also found that people who have a purpose in life tend to sleep better – and as we all know, the quality of our sleep can have an enormous impact on our general sense of wellbeing.

We start this book by looking at purpose because it is at the heart of the journey that lies ahead of us. Purpose is the first thing that we have to consider when we seek to improve our performance. When we understand our purpose, it becomes our North Star, offering direction and reassurance when we start to lose our way.

But do you really know what your purpose is? Too many of us sleepwalk through life's biggest decisions – we go to school, then perhaps an apprenticeship or university, we find a job, move into our own home, some of us start a family, then retire. It is only then that we start to think about ourselves and the things that make us truly happy.

We all know someone who has experienced a post-employment renaissance – the civil servant who took early retirement to start a business, or the parents who moved to a remote hobby farm after the kids had left the house. Ask any of these people if they have any regrets, and they will be quick to tell you that they just wish they had found their purpose sooner, so that they could have spent even more time living their best lives.

We owe it to ourselves to invest time and energy into figuring out our true purpose so that we can enjoy the rewards of a fulfilling life for as long as possible, and leave a positive legacy behind us.

By simply choosing to read this book, you have demonstrated a desire for self-improvement. That's the first step. We can now start the journey to confidence and success using real-life lessons and scientific evidence. And it all starts with a sense of purpose.

In order to discover our purpose, both experience and research show that we need to have three key components:

(1) Passion – what are you truly passionate about?
(2) Impact – what is the end goal?
(3) Community – what will your legacy be?

Passion represents the emotional connection that we have to our goals. This passion often begins in childhood, when we are inspired by an impressive role model and wish to emulate their success.

A young boy might look up to a beloved headteacher who once competed in the Olympics and won the respect and admiration of his community. This may inspire the boy to chase his own sporting dreams, igniting in him a passion for swimming that would carry him all the way to the London 2012 Olympics.

In this example, the impact or end goal is the win, and that win becomes the destination at the end of a long and difficult journey. It becomes our motivation – the thing that keeps us focused when we are inevitably faced with challenges.

But the win is not the end. In fact, it can become the inspiration for another person's purpose. A child watching the 2012 Olympics could watch the swimmers representing her country and vow to do the same one day. When she makes her debut at the LA 2028 Olympics, her achievements will only be possible because of the athletes who went before her. The impact that she makes will inspire a sense of purpose in the next generation, and on it goes.

These three components have been analysed and tested by scientists and academics as well as by sporting and business coaches, the military and many other organisations. The output of all these efforts from such diverse sources proves that success must always begin with a sense of purpose.

So it makes sense that we should all take some time to truly understand what our purpose actually is, and how we can leverage our existing passions and skills to achieve great things in our personal and professional lives.

It all begins with confidence – the confidence to take a thorough look at our lives and identify every weakness and strength; and the confidence which will aid us in realising our full potential.

1.2 DEFINING

Confidence as a concept is very hard to conceptualise as it is both emotional and cognitive. This means that it is both a feeling and a belief, and this is what makes it such a powerful tool. It is future-focused, founded on past experiences, and it gives us the motivation to keep going.

Confidence drives purpose, and purpose can be truly transformational.

For David Carry – a veteran of three Olympics, and a Commonwealth Games gold medalist - this transformation began in early childhood.

"I had a headteacher in my primary school who had competed in the 1960 Olympics," David says. "He was a local legend. His name was Ian Black and he was a triple gold medalist at the European Championships.

"In 1958 he was named BBC Sports Personality of the Year at the age of just 17, he was the youngest person ever to earn that title.

"I saw how respected he was in my local community and his daily presence in my school life made his achievements feel relevant. I have always loved to swim, but he showed me that it was possible to progress to the highest level in the world. And not only was it possible, but it was recognized and rewarded in many ways."

David's admiration of Ian Black gave him inspiration, motivation and an aspiration for the future.

In short, it gave him purpose. David went on to compete in three Olympics and three Commonwealth Games, winning numerous medals for his country before he retired in 2012. His achievements and his journey now serve as inspiration for a new generation of swimmers of all ages, giving them that same sense of purpose that pushed David to achieve his own goals.

We already know that in order to discover our purpose, we need to have three key components:

★ **Passion**

★ **Impact**

★ **Community**

Passion

Without passion, there is little point in setting a purpose. It is the thing that gets us up in the morning and the thing that keeps us going even when things are tough. Passion cannot be manufactured – it is a catalyst to create momentum. It exists deep within every one of us, and it is up to us to identify it and nurture it.

Impact

We all have an impact on the world around us in one way or another, but we don't always realise that we can choose the kind of impact that we make. Ask yourself where you want to end up? And taking that a step further, what legacy do you want to leave? When we sit by and do not choose the kind of impact we want to have, we often then blame external factors for our failures and shortcomings. We can have the ultimate impact when our passion is uninhibited by self-doubt. When we decide our impact from the outset, we can avoid falling into this common trap of justification, where our purpose is used as a weak justification for the life that we find ourselves in.

Community

A huge element of defining our purpose is knowing who we are going to serve. Who will our actions benefit?

This should not be treated as an afterthought, because used correctly, it can push us even further than we thought we could go. Many of us want to do something that's bigger than just us - we want to leave a legacy. Perhaps we want to inspire the next generation, as Ian Black inspired David Carry. Or perhaps we want to create something new and innovative within the business world. Or it may be that we simply don't want to let down our family.

When we have a strong understanding of the legacy we wish to create and the community that we are a part of and serve, that can generate a much bigger impact than simply working towards an individual goal could. Furthermore, when a purpose is defined really well it then becomes compelling and attracts other people to it.

1.3 SCIENCE AND EVIDENCE

Every high-achiever has a clear and defined purpose that has kept them focused and led them to success. We already know that purpose is the key component necessary for confidence and resilience.

In his TED talk and book "Start with Why", Simon Sinek (3) recounts some of the greatest achievements in history and points out that those who truly lead are able to create a following of people who act not because they were swayed by fear or obligation or perhaps bullied, but because they were inspired.

Act, Think and Communicate from the inside out

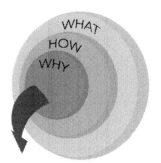

WHY - Your Purpose
Your motivation?
What do you believe?

HOW - Your Process
Specific actions taken
to realise your **WHY**

WHAT - Your Result
What do you do?
The result of **WHY**. Proof.

Figure 1.1 Adapted from Sinek's Golden Circle (3)

It is no accident that Sinek's Golden Circle mirrors the atomic structure, where 'Why' is at the heart (or nucleus) of everything we do. Sinek's 'How' represents the process by which we cultivate our identity, while his 'What' is the end result – the future state that we are all aspiring towards.

David Carry's 'Why' began in childhood when he realised he wanted to represent his country as an Olympic swimmer. His 'How' involved many years of hard work, training and sacrifice. His 'What' was a hugely successful career that saw him compete at the highest possible level of his chosen field. Or so he thought...

Again and again, we see how purpose is at the core of everything that we do. It offers guidance and a reminder that this is what we really care about, this is the thing we really love doing, and this is what we really want to achieve. And the more we are able to refine that, the more we believe that this is what we're here to do – and that provides the crucial emotional connection.

Once we are really sure about what it is that we care about and what we ultimately want to achieve, the more likely we are to actually go ahead and do it.

Numerous academic studies have looked at the power of purpose and how it can be applied to just about any ambition or goal. In a research paper titled "Vision and Mission in Organization: Myth or Heuristic Device?" (4) a series of academics concluded that "the impact of vision and mission statements on strategy cannot be overemphasized in the aspects of the performance of organization."

It is true that almost every business and organisation has its own mission statement or vision.

- Google's mission statement is "to organize the world's information and make it universally accessible and useful."
- Apple's mission statement is "to bring the best user experience to its customers through its innovative hardware, software, and services."
- BP's vision is "to have the best competitive corporate, operating and financial performance."

These mission statements act as a motivating factor, reminding employees what they are all working towards, and clarifying the overall purpose of their work.

In his seminal work 'Man's Search for Meaning'(5), Holocaust survivor and psychiatrist Viktor Frankl observed that the only way that people were able to outlast the horrors of the concentration camps was to find meaning in their lives, even when they were experiencing immense suffering. This theory – that human nature is motivated by the search for a life purpose – is now known as logotherapy, and it is practiced all across the world.

Logotherapy suggests that purpose can sometimes be discovered through disappointment and failure. This is something that Olympic athletes know all too well.

"In 2004 my whole dream was to make the Olympic Games and you want to have that moment of representing your country, wearing that tracksuit," says David. "I really did think that was the pinnacle. It was my dream as a kid.

"So 2004 came along and I made the swimming relay team, and I was just so happy to be there.

"We qualified for the finals of the 200m freestyle relay. I was the anchor leg, so I would be the last one to swim and it was my job to make sure that we got safely through to the end.

"So we completed the heats in the morning, and the finals were later on that day. We were a young squad of four guys who were all really excited about this opportunity to compete in the Olympic final and maybe even win a medal, and it was all going well until we had a team meeting.

"It was just an hour or two before the final session. We're all in the room and we're going through the session plan for the day. I was just about to head off and the team's lead performance director said: 'we've got a squad of six guys out here. They're here for the experience and there's real potential here, so we want all the guys to have a shot at swimming in that relay. So David, we're going to ask you to step to one side for this race."

"That moment was absolutely heartbreaking.

"As much as I wanted to pick up a chair and have a tantrum and throw it against the wall, that was not the best thing for the team. So I bit my tongue, sat on my hands and let it all play out and it turned out that those guys swam a really impressive swim. They broke the British record, but they missed a medal by less than one second.

"What was even more galling was that just a couple of weeks earlier, I had been swimming at a time that would have won us that medal and that really was a horrible feeling.

"I did not want to end my career like that and I never wanted that to happen again. So I really dedicated myself to training. For the next few years, I thought about nothing other than winning a medal as part of the relay team.

"In 2006, halfway through that four-year phase in between the Athens Olympics in 2004 and the Beijing Olympics in 2008, I won a couple of gold medals at the Commonwealth Games, as did a teammate of mine who was in that relay squad as well.

"So we were really on track and thinking we had a great chance at an Olympic medal. At this point in my life, winning that medal was what got me out of bed in the morning. I genuinely thought that it was my purpose in life to win an Olympic gold medal, and that's what I was driving towards.

"We made it to 2008 and again we qualified for the relay finals. Each one of us performed incredibly well. I got a personal best time, and we beat our target time as a team.

"But after all the stress and sacrifice and hard work over the previous four years, once again we missed the medal by less than one second. It was history repeating itself. But the pain I felt in 2008 was very different from my experience in 2004, because at least in 2008 I was actually given the chance to compete. I couldn't imagine a different outcome if I had been a part of the relay team because I was a part of it, and I knew I performed at my best.

"There was that sudden realisation that I was purposeless. I had no purpose in life. All I wanted was to win that medal and at that point, I was struggling to understand who I was, and what I was all about.

"That was a horrible feeling – way worse than not having a medal. And I very quickly realised that actually, the medal itself is not that relevant. It really is just a piece of metal that will one day end up sitting in a drawer. It has no intrinsic meaning.

"So that was really the beginning of my realisation that what I had been striving towards was not a medal, it was a win.

"However, it probably took around two weeks for that to really sink in. I spent those weeks after the 2008 Olympics dealing with the most profound disappointment – I had failed to achieve the one thing that I had spent four years training for.

"When the clouds lifted, I was able to look back and see that I had actually lived an incredible life over the past four years, but I just hadn't been aware of it. I had been able to pursue my passion for swimming, I won gold at the Commonwealth Games, I travelled the world and I represented my country at the highest level. But I had been in this tunnel visioned world where all that mattered was a medal.

"I went to my parents' house in Scotland to decompress and I remember being out in the garden. I decided to build this sort of observation deck that was strung between two trees. It's still there today.

"When I had finished it, I sat on the deck and looked around me at the beautiful Scottish fields and I thought 'Well, I actually really enjoyed that! That was an achievement.'

"Creating that deck was something that I really could feel proud of even though only a handful of people have actually seen it. That helped me to realise that there is definitely more to life than chasing medals.

"I have thought a lot about that race in 2008, and there were a lot of reasons why I didn't win. The beauty about sport is that there's no hiding place – there is only that key moment of realisation where you learn that you are not necessarily the person you thought you were. Not only did I not win in 2008, but actually I didn't even get close to my potential.

"I thought I really had performed at my best, but I could have done so much more. So there was a real drive to find out why the result didn't go the way I wanted.

"It wasn't necessarily the experience of Beijing 2008 that helped me to discover my purpose, it was the experience that followed it, when I was able to identify my values and the impact that I wanted to make.

"At that moment, I realised that there had to be something more, and that triggered my journey to figure out what else is out there and how I could be my best.

"If I were to reflect back on my experiences within sports, the experiences I'm most proud of are the ones where that challenge has been really high, when I've been doing something I really loved with people I really cared about, to achieve something really audacious."

David learned that his purpose was not necessarily a destination, it was a journey. By pinning all his hopes on a piece of metal, he risked missing the myriad opportunities that presented themselves to him along the way. His ultimate 'win' was a lot more profound than a moment on a podium, and it is a purpose that endures to this day through his work as a Track Record coach and Team Scotland ambassador.

REFERENCES

(1)   Steptoe, A., Deaton, A., and Stone, A. (2014). Subjective wellbeing, health, and ageing. The Lancet. 2015 (cited August 2019). Volume 385, issue 9968, p.640-648. Available from: https://www.thelancet.com/journals/lancet/article/PIIS0140-6736(13)61489-0/fulltext.

(2)   Espie, C et al (2018) Effect of digital cognitive behavioral therapy for insomnia on health, psychological well-being, and sleep-related quality of life: a randomized clinical trial. JAMA Psychiatry. 2019.(cited August 2019). Volume 76, No.1. Available from: https://jamanetwork.com/journals/jamapsychiatry/article-abstract/2704019?resultClick=1

(3)   Sinek, S. (2009). Start with Why: How Great Leaders Inspire Everyone to Take Action. London: Penguin Group. P.37-51

(4)   Taiwo, Akeem, Fatai Alani, Edwin M, (2016). Vision and Mission in Organization: Myth or Heuristic Device? The International Journal of Business & Management. Vol. 4. Issue 3. P. 127.

(5)   Frankl, Viktor. (2004). Man's Search for Meaning. 6th edition. Reading. Ebury Publishing.

1.4 HOW TO APPLY

At Track Record, the first thing we ask our clients to do is to write down their story, from passion to impact. This may sound obvious, but by writing down a win it becomes a commitment. By sharing this win with others, it becomes even more tangible, and the commitment deepens.

Exercise: The Track Record so far

Using the timeline, map of all your biggest accomplishments and failures – the positive experiences go above the line (the higher they are placed, the more significant they are) and the negative experiences go below the line (the lower they are placed, the worse that moment was).

Once we have this information, we can start to pull out the meaning. Look at the key experiences in your life and think about how they made you feel. Did you feel happiness and pride when you received your university degree? What made that experience so special? Was it the feeling of having worked hard to accomplish a goal? Of being able to pursue a particular career? Or overcoming financial or personal obstacles?

Likewise, look at the negative moments that have been identified. For instance, being overlooked for a promotion. Why was this such a negative experience? Was there a sense of unfairness at play? Or was it simply a case of not having worked hard enough?

Once we have looked at these formative experiences, we can start looking for connections and exploring the patterns. These were the moments that significantly impacted our world view, and it is these experiences that shaped our sense of reality. So the patterns that we start to pull out across the timeline have the potential to increase our self-awareness in terms of the choices we make, and perhaps help us to understand our purpose in life, at work, or in sport.

Next, we take a look into the future. It is your 80th birthday party and you are holding a huge celebration where you are celebrating the various successes that you have experienced throughout your life.

Exercise: Your Track Record to come

Where is the celebration being held?	
What is the venue?	
Who is in the room?	
How do your guests feel about you?	
How do you feel about your guests?	
What are the three things that you want to be able to mention in your 80th birthday party speech?	

This is a simple visualisation exercise that is a great way to identify the values and achievements that are actually important to us. By placing ourselves in the future and looking back, we can take a new look at our purpose and how it can be harnessed to bring us fulfilment and success.

It all goes back to having a heightened awareness of who we are, the impact that we can have on others and the impact that others have on us as well. With that alternative perspective, we can see things in a completely different light.

There's a lot of evidence that shows how our emotional intelligence can improve by doing these types of exercises because it's almost like watching a video replay of our lives – it gives us a different perspective of who we are, and allows us to see things that we have never seen before.

We can start to identify limiting patterns of behaviour, thinking traps like catastrophisation or turning opinions into facts. We are all guilty of doing these things, but in recognising them, we can become better people who can make clearer decisions.

Once we know our own stories, our purpose should become clear.

Exercise: Define your purpose

Passion	
What has consistently brought you the most joy in your life?	
Impact	
What, as an 80-year-old, did you identify that brought you most pride?	
Community	
Whose life will you have impacted in pursuit of your purpose?	
What do you consider to be your biggest achievement to date?	

Once we have identified those key moments and thought about why they were impactful, we can look for any patterns and how they've built up over time.

These exercises force us to reckon with our accomplishments, challenges, hopes and dreams. They help us to look towards our ideal future with a sense of purpose that will propel us closer to our end win.

Download the workbook for this chapter at: *WhatDoesItTakeToWin.com/workbook*

1.5 SUMMARY

There is a sense of purpose within us all, but in order to find it, we need to understand what drives us, what the accumulation of all our life's wins will achieve, and how we can use our sense of purpose to inspire ourselves and others, leaving a lasting legacy.

We also need to be aware that our sense of purpose can be heavily influenced by external factors and – in a way – by the thrill of the chase. For years, David believed that his purpose was to win an Olympic medal, before realising that it was simply to fulfil his purpose, passion and potential in each moment. Competing in three Olympic Games was a side effect of his purpose, and not the end goal itself.

Instead, our sense of purpose should be driven by our values and our identity – the core components of the self. By reviewing our historical accomplishments and disappointments we can gain an objective sense of what that identity really is, and this acts as a compass of sorts, keeping us on the right track even when external factors threaten to steer us off course.

We know that purpose is a vital component in our journey towards success and confidence. The value of purpose has been confirmed again and again in various academic papers and scientific studies, and the evidence is irrefutable. Whether we are operating as individuals or as team members in a large corporate organisation, a sense of purpose is required in order to press ahead and get that win. It is our mission statement and our motivator, and the foundation of our future success.

Chapter 2

Define your guiding values
– what do you stand for?

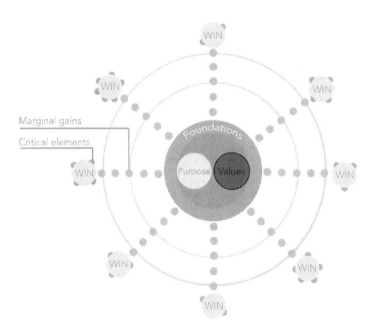

2.1 INTRODUCING VALUES

Our values act as our guiding principles which inspire us to be at our best. These values act as our conscience, keeping us on the right track, speeding up our decision making, and protecting our future selves from distraction.

In tandem with our purpose, they create the guardrails for the life we want to lead.

The American writer and runner George A. Sheehan once said: "Anything that changes your values changes your behaviour", and even a slight change in behaviour can make the difference between achieving that win or ending up disappointed.

We are still at the very beginning of this process – in the nucleus of the atom. The act of defining our values helps us to set our identity, and in tandem with our purpose, this will help to propel us towards our win.

We know from chapter 1 that confidence and success are driven by our values and identity, which embed in us a sense of purpose that can take us all the way to our goals, and beyond. Therefore, by dissecting and challenging our existing values, we can start making those behavioural changes which can give us that crucial edge that we need to press ahead and get that win.

But of course, the first step is to actually define our values. We can do this by taking a long and critical look at our priorities and asking ourselves why we have certain principles, and why they might be so important to us. Perhaps, our values reflect a religious upbringing or the influence of a mentor. Or maybe they represent our unique life experiences that have helped shape our views and outlook.

Sometimes it is easier to define our values in terms of what we don't believe – we may tell ourselves that we are not selfish. But as useful as this is, it is much more powerful to define our values in positive terms, even if this feels somewhat aspirational. For instance, rather than saying that we are 'not selfish', we may describe this value as 'generosity'. This value can easily be applied in a professional, sporting and personal setting, whether we are acting as individuals or as part of a team. By identifying this core value of generosity, we can free ourselves of the tyranny of indecision, and make proactive choices that turn these values into behaviours. To illustrate the point, a renowned musician may choose to turn down a lucrative gig in order to mentor a young singer. While that decision won't help the musician's own career in that particular moment, if it is in line with her value of generosity, it will help to move her towards her goal of giving back.

In this way, values can be incredibly powerful, and they can fill us with confidence. Values enable us to take a short cut on difficult decisions – they act as a filter, increasing in importance under pressure. By simply taking some time to examine ourselves and consider our aspirations, we can gain a sense of self-awareness that will sustain us throughout our journey to confidence and success.

2.2 DEFINING

Values are a part of our identity. They represent the things that are most important to us in life, and they drive every decision that we make. When we make decisions that are consistent with our values, we are happier and more confident in ourselves. When we make decisions and behave out of alignment with our values, life tends to be stressful and we feel unhappy, frustrated, lacking or incomplete.

"Men go abroad to wonder at the heights of mountains, at the huge waves of the sea, at the long courses of the rivers, at the vast compass of the ocean, at the circular motions of the stars, and they pass by themselves without wondering."
St Augustine

Values play such an important role in our journey towards confidence, yet most of us have never really had an opportunity to explore our true values and consider whether or not we are living a life which reflects our core beliefs.

So how do we set and understand our values?

Our values are created and sustained by our beliefs,

and these beliefs are influenced by our personal experiences in life, as well as the beliefs of the people who surround us. Our parents, family, teachers and friends can play a hugely significant role in helping us set our values and challenging any values that may not reflect our beliefs. Likewise, the media, pop culture and politics can play a role in shaping our values by reinforcing existing beliefs and introducing new ideas that may match our world view.

It is important to acknowledge that these external forces can play both a positive and negative role when it comes to setting and defining our values. It is ultimately our own responsibility to manage these influences and take the time to ensure that we are not drifting too far from the core of who we are. If one of our core values is integrity, and we say that we are not a smoker, but then we smoke a cigarette –our values and our behaviour are not in alignment and we are basing our values on a lie. Understanding our values is one of the foundations of self-awareness, and without self-awareness, we risk losing our way.

Sporting stars across the world use their value base as an inspirational tool to drive trust, confidence and performance. One of the best examples of this is the New Zealand All Blacks. As one of the most successful rugby teams of all time, the All Blacks have taken on a leadership role in their country, which has embedded the team in the culture and identity of the nation. This has been true for many decades, despite personnel changes in the team and the innumerable highs and lows that come with being an international sports team.

One of the ways in which the All Blacks communicate their values is through the iconic Haka ritual before each match. The Haka acts as a reminder of the players' roots by referencing New Zealand's history and indigenous culture. By performing the Haka just before a match, the All Blacks are reinforcing their shared bond and team values, right when it matters the most.

It is the common values of the team that makes the All Blacks such an extraordinary force, and this gives them unparalleled confidence – is it any wonder their opponents find this Haka ritual so intimidating? Imagine how powerful we could be if we all performed our own Haka ritual to focus on our values as a battle cry before a significant moment in our lives: a boardroom presentation; an exam; or an Olympic race.

In his book Legacy: What the All Blacks Can Teach Us About the Business of Life, James Kerr (1) says that by leaning on their team story, the All Blacks have been able to create meaning to their values and therefore accountability to live true to these values.

"In doing so, they are using [their values] as a lens for the behaviours within their culture," says Kerr. "Wouldn't it be amazing if your organisation could do the same?"

It doesn't matter if we are setting values for ourselves as individuals or as a team, the guiding principles are the same. If the purpose we identified in chapter 1 is our 'why', our values are the 'how' – they get us from a point of aspiration to action. Our behaviour should always be grounded in our values, so our values provide the lens through which we see the world. This can then allow us to make positive choices and even change the way we are perceived.

But there are no short cuts here. An honest person can't simply state that their values are honesty, and then draw a line under it. That approach is not going to lead to any personal growth or behavioural change. In order to claim honesty as a value, we must prioritise honesty above all else, choosing to be honest even when it might lead to some awkwardness.

We must embed our values into our identify, for it to become an intrinsic part of who we are. This makes the value much more meaningful and allows our behaviour to flow naturally from our core.

Our values should also challenge us and give us something to aspire to. If we say that one of our values is to be conscientious, then we may need to consider the ways in which we express this to other people. This may involve going out of our way to be more diligent in order to demonstrate our commitment to following through on what we said we would do. This may be time-consuming, and it may require an added time commitment and it could even tap into our reserves of patience, but if it is in service of an important value then we know that this time and effort will pay off in the end. The more we work on our core values and beliefs, the stronger they become.

Clash of values

We have all found ourselves trapped in a conversation about politics, religion, sports or art, where we hold completely divergent views to the person we are talking to. No matter how passionately we make our case, or how many sources we quote, we are not able to change our opponent's view at all. This is a classic clash of values – there may be no animosity behind the conversation, but it still feels threatening, as this person is challenging us to defend our values. If our values have not been defined, this can become an impossible task which leaves us feeling confused, conflicted and downright angry. This is why it is so important to work out whether you are experiencing a value clash, or whether your perception of someone else's behaviour is just plain wrong.

Katherine Moore spent ten years working with Olympic athletes as a physiotherapist and head of sports science. She knows that one of her core values is that she is true. Katherine values honesty in herself and others, and she lives this value by being true to herself and truthful in her actions. This is something that she values highly in herself and looks for in others. But this core value has been challenged again and again.

"I always remind people that behaviours don't define the person – values do," Katherine explains. "With values, things can get really emotional and people become very passionate quite quickly because they are so deeply connected to you. But you need to ask yourself, is this just behaviour I'm seeing or do I factually know that their belief is that they are simply not a 'true' person? Because they are two very different things.

"What sparked a change for me was when I had a really explicit conversation with someone who was very influential in the sport, to find out the facts about whether my perception of their values was true. And it was. At that point, I could honestly say 'That's great, but your values are so different to mine that I can't stay in this role.'

"It was really unemotive, it was a very factual conversation at that point because I knew what my drivers were and they were very clear about theirs. But up to that point it had been an emotionally draining situation for me, because I just couldn't make my mind up about whether the issue was their behaviour and my perception of it, or if we were simply not a good fit. Had I simply had the values conversation four years previously, there would have been a different outcome."

In this example, the ability to quickly identify a value clash would have saved Katherine frustration. When we work in a partnership or team where the core values are not aligned, it is just a matter of time before that causes an irreversible rupture. But values can be very hard for people to articulate, even after we have identified what those values may be. What may seem obvious in hindsight can feel impossible – and even irrelevant - at the time.

"Values are an adjective as opposed to a noun."
David Carry

Values are essentially descriptive and intangible, but they lead to real action and behavioural change. If we use our values as a lens, we can make them real through our everyday conduct and our relationships with others. By reinforcing our values through our behaviours, we show others that we have a true sense of our identity and that we are consistent. This builds trust and helps other people to understand the way we behave.

Say we have a colleague who holds the value that it is important to live with a sense of joy. They may express this by bringing humour to situations whenever they can, and by laughing a lot. But another colleague may perceive this attitude as messing around and not taking anything seriously, which could present a clash of values. But if both colleagues have an understanding of each other's values and why they are important to them, this can diffuse any potential conflict and actually build trust and respect instead.

By defining and living our values in this way, we are taking ownership of our identity and leaving no space for misinterpretation.

Core values versus aspirational values

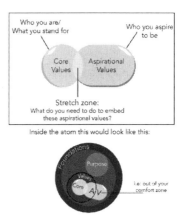

Figure 2.1 Core and aspirational values

As depicted in the figure 2.1 above we have both core values and aspirational values, important, but distinctly different.Our core values are embedded deep within us. They are the things we do that are integral to us. Think about the words that people would use to describe you

– maybe you are a loyal person, a kind person, or an unflappable person. These are core values that require little effort to maintain.

Then there are our aspirational values. Consider your future self at the moment of the win – what values do you need to have at that moment, which may be challenging for you right now? Let's say, your win involves becoming chief executive of a FTSE 100 company. Your primary role will be to lead a global team of thousands, many of whom you will never meet.

You will therefore need to be able to inspire and galvanise this entire organisation, and to create a sense of connection with your employees so they feel linked to the purpose of the organisation and everything that you are all doing.

By telling yourself "I am an inspirational leader", you are challenging yourself to embody this role and everything that comes with it. You will need to analyse how you interact with the business and its stakeholders, to develop a clear communication style, to find a way to measure your impact, and to hold yourself to account. Keep telling yourself and others that you are an inspirational leader until it becomes difficult for you to act in any other way.

Katherine's story

Track Record's head coach Katherine Moore knows that one of her core values is curiosity, because she is a naturally curious person. But that natural curiosity is not going to help her reach her full potential in life. So she started to think about the ways in which she could use her curiosity to propel her forward in life.

"I realised that I am a learner," she said. "That was one of my aspirational values. The active declaration that 'I am a learner' was very different from the passive realisation that 'I am a curious person'. It forced me to push myself into some scary places.

"I realised that if I was going to be a learner, I needed

27

to embody that value and be challenged by that. I decided to start taking on feedback better, and I started to say yes to things that I would have otherwise said no to.

"My four-year-old son has started karate lessons, and the teacher runs a mixed class for parents and children. The teacher asked me if I would prefer to stand at the back while my son practiced – and the old me would have loved to just sit back and watch! But I knew that if I was really going to embody the fact that I am a learner, then saying no to new experiences wouldn't fit with that. So, I joined the class, and now my son and I both have our blue belts together."

Katherine discovered the importance of owning our values. If your shortlist includes the words curiosity, creativity and trustworthiness, take ownership of these values by stating:

"I am a learner"
"I am a creator"
"I am somebody who can be trusted"

In his book Atomic Habits (2), James Clear writes about the importance of embodying habits in your identity, and it is the same for values. Rather than saying 'learning is my value', claim it for yourself by stating 'I am a learner'. Speak these values, write them down, and remind yourself of them until they are embedded in your subconscious and your behaviour effortlessly reflects your values.

2.3 SCIENCE AND EVIDENCE

"Every one of us has in him a continent of undiscovered character. Blessed is he who acts the Columbus to his own soul." Anonymous

The themes of value and identity have been analysed since the dawn of thought – as a species, humans have an endless need to understand the world around us. Yet we are frequently thwarted by our own inability to take a critical look at ourselves. The discovery of our values is a discovery of self, while recognition of another person's values can help us to gain a better insight into the people who surround us.

"The recognition of differences is so important," says Hannah MacLeod, Olympic gold medallist with the Great Britain hockey team. "Taking the time to understand other people's values and recognising the strengths that come from those values is really important.

"When you receive criticism in a certain way, sometimes you may find that it sparks an emotive response that is quite unexpected. Often, this is because the criticism is really specific to one of your core values. By understanding our core values, we can gain a better understanding of our reaction to situations. For example, one of my core values is respect for self and others, and as soon as I see someone else being disrespected, I get incredibly angry.

"It took me a long time to understand why that was the case. I just got really upset. And I thought, it's no big thing, but it really got to me. It was later on when I took the time to go through that process that I realised why I got so emotional. It was because respect was so important to me. That helped me to process it much quicker and have an understanding about how to get a sense of control back, and give meaning to that emotion, which is something a lot of people struggle with."

Hannah's experience has been reflected in academic

research. Researchers are fascinated by the idea that simply by setting our values, we can gain a huge amount of control over the direction of our lives, while also becoming happier, more successful people.

In a paper titled 'The role of values and value congruence for job satisfaction, person organisation fit, work, engagement and resilience' Megan Frances Bissett (3), argues that one of the most common proven outcomes of value congruence is job satisfaction. If an individual has minimal conflict between their own personal values and the organisations' values it will result in positive outcomes for both the individual and the organisation.

This view is echoed by the leadership expert Richard Barrett. In his paper 'The Importance of Values in Building a High Performance Culture' (4) he states that when we work in an organisation where the culture aligns with our personal values, "we feel liberated".

"Unleashing this energy is tantamount to liberating the corporate soul," he adds.

Barrett has experienced this theory first hand through his work with more than 2,000 large companies in the public and private sectors in more than 60 different countries.

"Our experience...allows us to state categorically that values-driven organisations are the most successful organisations on the planet," he says.

Figure 2.2 demonstrates how this works.

In the private sector:
Values and behaviours drive culture Culture drives employee fulfilment Employee fulfilment drives customer satisfaction Customer satisfaction drives shareholder value
In the public sector:
Values and behaviours drive culture Culture drives employee fulfilment Employee fulfilment drives mission assurance Mission assurance drives customer satisfaction

Figure 2.2 How values drive business success

In both the private and public sectors, values are at the root of organisational success. But the same rule also applies for personal and sporting success. Over the past 20-plus years, a significant amount of research has been conducted to look specifically at the consequences of personal values in various cultures.

Confidence, in essence, is the extent to which we believe we have control over the choices we make, and how much we trust that these choices and our actions can increase our chances of success" – Track Record

The concept of the 'locus of control' was identified as early as 1954 by the psychologist Julian Rotter (5), who described it as the extent to which people believe they have power over events in their lives.

At Track Record, we have found that individuals with an internal locus of control tend to have greater confidence in their ability to influence outcomes through their own actions. The ability to exert control over one's own motivation, behaviour, and social environment is an incredibly powerful tool in the journey towards confidence. These beliefs influence the goals for which people strive, the amount of energy expended toward goal achievement, and likelihood of attaining particular levels of behavioural performance.

Individuals with high self-efficacy typically have an internal locus of control, which allows them to have greater control over any given situation. Research suggests that the locus of control is related to a transformational leadership style and that an internal locus of control is the preferable orientation for successful leadership (6). In the Track Record PERFORM methodology, an internal locus of control is defined as a "Winning Mindset" and an external locus of control is defined as a "Victim Mindset." A victim mindset is not going to get us far when we are actively pursuing a win.

According to Sagiv et al, in the thesis 'Personal Values in Human Life' (7), self-reported values can actually predict a large variety of attitudes, preferences and overt behaviours.

"Individuals act in ways that allow them to express their important values and attain the goals underlying them," the thesis states. "Thus, understanding personal values means understanding human behaviour."

Values are who we are, but they are also aspirational goals that we set for ourselves: we want to be seen as a reliable team member, so we view reliability as a desirable quality that we praise in others and cultivate within ourselves. Over time, the value turns into a behaviour, and we become known as being a reliable person, who is true to themselves.

This is a particularly useful advantage to have in the workplace, where the right values can help an employee to gain seniority in an organisation without ever losing their sense of self. Of course, this journey is even easier when the organisation's values align with our personal values, which makes it all the more important to choose the right career path and the right workplace. In this chapter, we have seen a few examples of how value alignment can have a 'make or break' effect.

We owe it to ourselves to waste no time defining and testing our values so that we can go on to reach our full potential and lead our most fulfilling lives.

Similarly, by taking the time to understand other people's values, we can improve our relationships considerably, and reduce conflict in the long term.

REFERENCES

(1)   Kerr, James (2013), Legacy: What the All Blacks Can Teach Us About the Business of Life. London: Constable & Robinson.

(2)   Clear, James (2018). Atomic Habits. New York: Random House Business.

(3)   Bissett, Megan Frances (2014), The role of values and value congruence for job satisfaction, person organisation fit, work, engagement and resilience. Masters dissertation for University of Canterbury Christchurch, New Zealand. Available at: https://core.ac.uk/download/pdf/35470944.pdf. [viewed June 2019].

(4)   Barrett, Richard (2010), The Importance of Values in Building a High-Performance Culture. Barrett Values Centre. Available at: https://www.valuescentre.com/wp-content/uploads/PDF_Resources/Additional_Articles/Article_Importance_of_Values.pdf. [viewed June 2019].

(5)   Rotter, Julian B (1966). "Generalized expectancies for internal versus external control of reinforcement". Psychological Monographs: General and Applied. 80: P.1–28.

(6)   Burns, J.M. (1978). Leadership. New York: Harper and Row

(7)   Sagiv, Lilach and Roccas, Sonia (2017), Personal Values in Human Life. Nature Human Behaviour. August 2017 Issue. Available at: https://www.researchgate.net/publication/319269391_Personal_values_in_human_life. [viewed June 2019].

2.4 HOW TO APPLY

We understand the huge significance of value recognition as a tool for success, but how do we actually identify and live our values?

First, think about how we choose to define ourselves when we are introduced to a new person for the first time. The first two questions are generally: what is your name, and what do you do? What do your answers say about you? Do they reflect your values? It's unlikely that your name will have much of an impact on your personal values, but your job tells a different story.

We spend most of our adult life at work, and so it is inevitable that we come to be defined by the person we are in the office, or the job we choose to do. This is particularly true for professional athletes. Earlier in this chapter, we referred to Hannah MacLeod not simply as 'Hannah MacLeod', but as 'Hannah MacLeod, Olympic gold medallist'.

By grouping her name and career accomplishments together, her comments gain more relevance and command attention. One of Hannah's core values is respect, and she was able to use that as a motivation to propel herself forward and reach the pinnacle of her career. But it was not enough for her to simply value respect – she lived this value by training hard, respecting her talents, and dedicating herself to her team. As an Olympic gold medallist and internationally-ranked hockey player, she now has the respect of millions of people, thus reinforcing and rewarding her commitment to her core value.

How can you convert your values into life, career or sporting success? Start by taking a pen and paper and answering the following questions.

1. In the last six months, what has been your strongest response to an event or person, positive or negative?

2. What caused it?
3. Which value did it involve?
4. Did this represent a value clash?
5. What did you learn from it?

The answers to these questions will help to determine our core values. Now think about the future.

6. Consider the people you will interact with in the future – who are they?
7. How do you wish to be seen and spoken about by others?
8. How do you want to feel in ten years' time?

These questions can help us to identify our aspirational values – the things that we would like to be when we view ourselves in the future.

Consider your hopes and dreams, and make a list of the aspirational values that will challenge you to live up to your potential. For example, these may include:

- Honesty
- Efficiency
- Curiosity
- Reliability
- Creativity
- Confidence
- Innovation
- Trustworthiness
- Loyalty
- Commitment
- Kindness

Make a long list, then order each of these aspirational values according to priority. Take away any values that aren't very important to you. Then as a final priority check, ask yourself to choose between values. For instance: would you rather have respect than laughter? Physical fitness or academic prowess? Independence or a large family?

Keep going through this list until you have just three or four aspirational values left. They should be roughly in alignment with your core values, so that you are never trying to be someone that you're not.

Then consider how you can embed them into your identity. this could be through adding "I am" before the value – for instance, "I am a learner". This will help you to imagine what life would be like when you truly live your values, and how they can affect your everyday behaviours and responses.

Download the workbook for this chapter at: *WhatDoesItTakeToWin.com/workbook*

2.5 SUMMARY

It can be hard to connect the idea of defining our values with professional and personal success, but the evidence linking these is clear. Athletes and executives have been practising the value-to-success ritual for years and it is a tried and tested way to both understand ourselves and encourage self-improvement.

By investing just a little time to define and set our values, we are protecting our future selves from disappointment and conflict. The more we understand ourselves, the easier our lives will be. Faced with a difficult decision, we simply have to ask ourselves: does this align with my values? If there is no clear answer to that question, then it may be time to revisit those core values and see if anything has changed.

Our values tell us what we stand for, what we hold precious, and what is deserving of our limited energy reserves. We may even become so familiar with our values that they can practically predict our response in certain situations. This helps to build trust and security within our closest relationships, and it helps to minimise the risk that we may be expected to act or react in a way that does not sit well with our value base.

A strong foundation of values is one of the greatest gifts we can give ourselves – we just have to put the work in and keep reminding ourselves of our defining qualities until our behaviour falls in line and we learn to live with complete confidence in ourselves and our ability to succeed.

Chapter 3

Select your foundations
- What is most important?

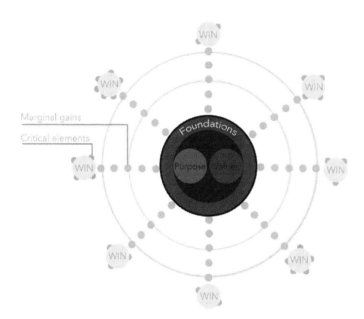

3.1 INTRODUCING FOUNDATIONS

In the atomic confidence model, our foundations encircle our purpose and identity, cementing them and creating a strong core for our atomic confidence. They offer a practical push from idea to win, by helping us to make useful, meaningful changes in our daily life and to build good habits. This starts with an understanding of our energy and time limitations.

Every person's energy is finite, so how are you choosing to spend yours? We all make hundreds of tiny choices each day that define our priorities and use up our daily ration of energy. How we choose to spend our energy can make the difference between a focused, successful person and a disorganised person who is living day to day.

Athletes come up against this issue all the time. There are multiple examples of high-level athletes being forced to make tough choices in order to get the win, from the cyclist who has to make a difficult decision to factor in her recovery, to the swimmer who has to push past the boredom of a mid-week session in order to find the value in it.

The same rules apply in business as well. Time management is now a given in any workplace, but by managing our energy we can be even more productive and fulfilled, becoming better employees and business-owners.

In his 2007 article 'Performing a Project Pre-mortem' (1), Gary Klein talks about the benefits of "prospective hindsight". The pre-mortem looks at all the potential delays, distractions and environmental issues that might get in the way of completing a project. By identifying these problems, we can look ahead and strengthen our plans to minimise the risk of a disaster. This then allows us to pour our energy into the task at hand, rather than seeing it get sapped by numerous diversions that could have been handled ahead of time.

Too often we become victims of our inability to prior-itise energy management; complaining about spending time on non-productive tasks without acknowledging that we are ultimately in control of our own time and energy. We answer the phone as we are rushing to leave the house, making us five minutes late for our next appointment. We stay up late when we know we have an early meeting in the morning, making us tired and less focused. We underperform in a race because we did not give ourselves enough time to train. These are all problems which could have been solved by pre-emptive action, but without a strong foundation base, we risk missing some obvious opportunities for self-improvement.

Our foundations are the areas of focus in our lives where we consciously choose to spend time and energy. When we choose our foundations, we are confirming our priorities and establishing our goals. We are able to focus on the things that really matter to us and redirect all of our energy in the direction of success.

When Olympic swimmer David Carry spent some time thinking about his foundations, he realised they were relatively straightforward: family and friends, his career both swimming and post swimming, and his wellbeing.

"When I know that those three things are in place, then I'm more likely to make better decisions, and decisions that are closer to my purpose and achieving my win," he says.

By making this realisation, he was able to prioritise these three elements and cut out all the other things that were holding him back.

3.2 DEFINING

Our foundations are the areas of our life which are most important to us. They are the activities and rituals that we choose to prioritise in order to be more effective, successful people. Once we are aware of the strength of our foundations, we can use them to help us direct our time and energy more efficiently, with minimal waste.

When we actively choose our foundations, we also eliminate the things which are less important to us. This allows us to minimise any distractions and focus purely on what it is that we are working towards – our wins.

Understanding what is important to us and where to

focus our time is an essential part of the confidence process. It leads to a sense of identity of who we really are. We can encourage this sense of identity by making choices about where we spend our time and who we spend our time with. For instance, a cyclist training for the Olympics would give himself a much better chance of winning a medal if he spent most of his time at the track with a trainer or teammate. But in order to do this, he may need to sacrifice some precious family time – at least until The Games are over. Likewise, the owner of an ice cream shop may choose to forego a summer holiday in order to benefit from a seasonal rush that will bring more money into the business. And a parent may choose to skip a work meeting in order to be there for their child during a particularly dreaded exam.

Think of energy like a battery. We can expend that energy any way we wish, but there is only a limited store that we can take from before we run out of power. How do we best distribute that energy?

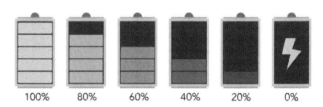

Energy is like a battery

In order to do this, we have to differentiate between time and energy. Most of us understand that time is a resource, but how we choose to spend our time can have a huge impact on our battery power. It is possible to spend a lot of time with a person and increase our overall energy, or even add to our energy reserves. Such as, a session with a life coach, business mentor or personal trainer may leave us feeling focused and energised.

Likewise, there are some people who can deplete our energy stores by taking our time for granted, such as a friend who is always late. When we are working towards a set win, any time wasted can represent a major setback, so we have to take a highly disciplined approach towards our time management.

As we can see in figure 3.1, our day is split into three different types of energy: energy generating activities; energy depleting activities; and performance enhancement activities.

Energy and Time

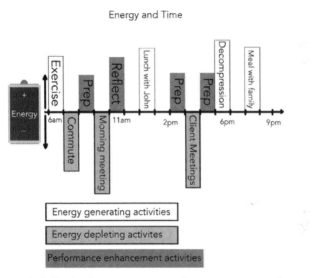

Figure 3.1 Each day contains a finite amount of time and energy

We show respect for our limited free time by eliminating negative thought patterns and reminding ourselves that these are the foundations that we have selected - if we don't use them to build our best lives, we are only failing ourselves.

If we tell ourselves we don't have time to go to the gym because we have to work late, that's a choice that we are making. If the end goal is to get a promotion, then choosing work over the gym is the right thing to do in order to accomplish that win. But if the end goal is weight loss or improved fitness, then we are losing the focus on our win by spending our limited time and energy doing overtime at work instead of going to the gym.

Being able to choose how we expend our energy is a critical element of confidence. That's because it allows us to spend time and energy in the areas where we think are going to make the most impact. That impact will be to get us faster, better, closer to that ultimate win.

However, it is worth remembering that not all goals have to be as all-consuming as an Olympic medal. Arianna Huffington's 12 Steps to Thrive (2) have struck a chord with busy millennials and stressed-out workers who are struggling to achieve the perfect work/ life balance. She offers obvious advice such as getting more sleep and exercise, along with joy-inspiring activities such as keeping a gratitude list and picking an image that ignites creativity.

While Huffington's 12 steps offer some great tips for a balanced life, when it comes to creating confidence and working towards a win, the list is much shorter.

In order to set strong foundations, we need to identify our own 'steps to thrive', and then live them. For David Carry, it can all be boiled down to three key things: nutrition, recovery and exercise. And you don't have to be an Olympian to benefit from them.

Nutrition
We often accept nutritional care as a given for elite athletes, then fail to make that connection to ourselves. But good nutrition is an extension of having a good mindset, it is about making better choices that enable us to be consistent in our performance and to maximise our energy potential.

What we consume can have a significant effect on our lifestyles and our ability to succeed. A lot of people fall into the trap of skipping meals, eating at their desks, or loading up on quick snacks and meals that are high in sugar, salt or complex carbohydrates. Sugary foods cause the blood pressure to spike, creating a momentary surge of energy followed by a much longer slump. Needless to say, this pattern is not conducive to a productive working environment.

Even something as simple as hydration can help – most of us do not drink enough water in a day and dehydration can lead to energy lapses. Likewise, whole, clean, protein-rich food is always going to be better than ready-meals or pre-packaged snacks.

Then extend the theory of good nutrition to encompass cultural and social aspects as well. We are all guilty of consuming too much negative news, which can lead to low-level anxiety and a reduction in energy. We can avoid the worst of this by switching off news notifications and limiting the amount of time spent browsing news sites and social media, time that could be spent on more positive and productive activities instead.

Recovery

At least four of Arianna Huffington's 12 Steps (2) relate to rest, and the benefits of recovery time cannot be underestimated.

Good quality sleep is non-negotiable, as tired people simply have less energy. We could all stand to improve our quality of sleep by making a few easy lifestyle changes. Excessive caffeine and alcohol consumption are known to disrupt sleep, while the blue light emitted from smartphones, laptops and iPads can disrupt the natural sleep-wake cycle, making it harder to fall asleep.

Another one of Arianna Huffington's tips is to "turn off your devices" and "escort them out of the bedroom", this is a small but significant change that we can all make today that will have a positive impact on tomorrow's performance.

But recovery does not begin and end with a good night's sleep. It can mean taking time to meditate or to

45

reflect on the day's activities. It could be time spent in a sauna or steam room after a particularly tough workout. Or it could be taking some time to get closer to nature, away from the hustle and bustle of modern life.

Recovery time allows us to rest and reset, so we can keep pushing ourselves forward without risk of burnout.

Exercise

Just as an athlete has to train before a competitive event, we all have to practice our performance so we can get better and faster over time. Stress levels are continuous in the business world, especially during times when resources and time are limited.

It's very easy to get into the mindset of feeling that life is a marathon performance where we just have to keep going and going in order to, hopefully, get to where we need to be, or at least make it to the weekend. However, the concept of 'sprint, rest, and repeat' can be much more effective when we have a particular goal in mind. When we sprint, we are operating at maximum capacity, with speed, agility and focus. When the sprint is done, we rest and recover before doing it all again.

This is the mindset that we need to bring to our working life in order to meet our goals head-on.

Most of us are not putting our bodies into physically draining situations, but the unconscious, cognitive loading of a day can easily become an energy-sapping routine. By switching our focus from the marathon to the sprint, we can avoid the threat of apathy and be our best more often.

3.3 SCIENCE AND EVIDENCE

Time management is a common concept in most workplaces, but energy management arguably offers a better approach.

In their 2007 thesis 'Manage Your Energy, Not Your

Time', Tony Schwartz and Catherine McCarthy (3) tested the idea of energy management at the US-based Wachovia Bank, and the results spoke for themselves.

The pair took one group of employees through a pilot energy management program which focused specific strategies for increasing capacity and maximising their energy. These strategies were embedded in their routines over a four-month period. Schwartz and McCarthy then measured their job performance against that of a control group.

The employees who took part in the program were given four key areas of focus: the body, the emotions, the mind and the human spirit.

The body: physical energy
Participants were encouraged to adopt lifestyle changes that improved their awareness of exercise, diet and sleep patterns. One Wachovia executive overhauled his eating habits, began regular cardiovascular and strength training and started going to bed at a designated time and sleeping longer. He lost 50 pounds during the four-month period and found that he was more focused and had more energy throughout the day.

The emotions: quality of energy
A busy life can put the body into 'fight or flight' mode – a high-energy, short-term effect that leaves us feeling exhausted, impatient and anxious. To avoid entering this mode, participants were taught how to 'buy time' by exhaling slowly for five or six seconds every time they started to feel stressed out. This is all it takes to induce relaxation and recovery and avoid falling into 'fight or flight' patterns. One participant - Sony Europe president Fujio Nishida – found that this ritual was so effective he was able to quit smoking.

The mind: focus of energy

Distractions can be costly, so participants were asked to start using "ultradian sprints" to improve their concentration. This involves completely focusing on work for 90-120 minutes, then taking a break, then moving on to another activity for another 90-120 minutes.

One E&Y executive realised that a constant stream of emails was interrupting his focus throughout the day. So he created a ritual of checking his e-mail just twice a day—at 10:15am and 2:30pm. He spent 45 minutes at a time answering his emails, and he was able to clear his inbox every day.

The human spirit: energy of meaning and purpose

If the work that we are doing aligns with our personal values, we are likely to take more satisfaction and meaning from our jobs. This can lead to better focus and greater perseverance in the workplace. To benefit from this positive energy, we need to identify our core values and stay true to them on a daily basis, as well as consciously allocating energy to the important areas of our lives – our family, our health (self care), our work and social.

This can be harder than it seems, we may think that we are allocating our time equally among these four different areas, but when we actually track our time and energy we realise we can find we are actually spending substantially more time on work and socialising than we are on our family and self care. This could mean that we are passively prioritising work and social life in a way that does not necessarily reflect our values and will not help us reach our end win.

When we identify our foundations and manage our time accordingly, we give ourselves the best possible chance of succeeding.

This was ultimately proven in the Wachovia Bank case study. The employees who took part in the energy management program outperformed the controls on a series of workplace metrics, such as the value of loans they generated, as you can see in figure 3.3.

Percentage increase in **loan** revenues*

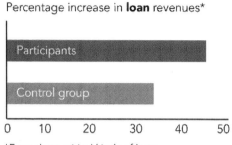

*From three critical kinds of loans

Percentage increase in **deposit** revenues

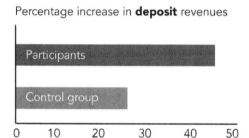

Figure 3.2 Reprinted by permission of Harvard Business Review. Exhibit from "Manage Your Energy, Not Your Time" by Schwartz, Tony and McCarthy, Catherine, October 2007. Copyright © 2019 by Harvard Business Publishing; all rights reserved.

This study showed how energy management substantially increased productivity, helping Wachovia's employees to become even more successful in their careers.

The study concluded that "people can cultivate positive emotions by learning to change the stories they tell themselves about the events in their lives.

"Often, people in conflict cast themselves in the role of victim, blaming others or external circumstances for their problems. Becoming aware of the difference between the facts in a given situation and the way we interpret those facts can be powerful in itself.

"It's been a revelation for many of the people we work with to discover they have a choice about how to view a given event and to recognise how powerfully the story they tell influences the emotions they feel. We teach them to tell the most hopeful and personally empowering story possible in any given situation, without denying or minimising the facts."

A similar theory was floated in 1989 by a group of US-based academics (4). They found that by asking their subjects to imagine that an event has already occurred, those subjects could increase their ability to identify any potential issues by up to 30%. Gary Klein calls this a 'premortem', and it is another example of the value of good energy management as a means of increasing productivity and reducing time wasting.

The ability to foresee potential obstacles allows us to take early preventative action so we do not have to expend unnecessary energy on activities that are not going to help us reach our goals. For instance, two people buy a home together and start to think about any issues that could negatively impact them in the future. They realise that they are living at the edge of a flood zone and estimate that their existing home insurance will not cover the cost of any small valuables that were being kept on the ground floor. They invest in a waterproof safe for their passports, birth certificates and jewellery and keep it out of harm's way on the second floor of the house. This small change will remove the risk of losing a cherished necklace or vital document in the future.

More importantly, by choosing to value our time and energy in this way, we are demonstrating a high level of respect for our goals and reinforcing the foundational values that we have worked so hard to create.

Setting priorities

Setting priorities is one of those things that seems obvious on paper but can be very hard to actually implement in real life. It requires drive and commitment, and most importantly – support.

As a coach and performance scientist for British Cycling at the 2008 and 2012 Olympics, Scott Gardner had to encourage the athletes to make some tough choices about how they chose to spend their energy.

"There's a real honesty required with the self if you want to be the best," says Scott.

"I remember prior to Beijing 2008, working with eventual gold medallist Jamie Staff. This guy was 34 and he had two kids and a wife, but he wasn't truly being honest with himself about what he had to do in order to achieve his Olympic ambition.

"When you're an athlete, recovery between training is crucial and therefore you need to rest a lot, and he was a really conscientious guy when it came to his family life. With team support, Jamie looked at his life closely and thoroughly explored all of his foundations, with recovery being one.

"He was going home after training and helping around the house, maybe making dinners, cleaning up, doing active stuff with the kids – he was doing a brilliant job of being a dad, but he wasn't doing a brilliant job of being an athlete because he wasn't resting, therefore he wasn't recovering.

"As a consequence, Jamie wasn't adapting to training optimally and at the age of 34, he was really struggling to do what was required to win. It took some real honesty from himself and some really hard conversations with his family about the sacrifice that would be required over the next eighteen months in order to reach their goals. That included a lot more rest.

"Most of us might think that this involves going home to sit on the couch and be lazy, but what he was doing was going home, sitting on the couch and recovering so that he could train optimally again tomorrow.

"It wasn't going to be like that for the rest of his life, but for that particular year, he had to conserve his energy for training so that he would have the best chance of winning at the Olympic Games.

"He knew he wasn't resting enough, and with team support he was able to make that change amongst others, and he went on to win an Olympic gold medal and do the fastest time ever at an Olympic Games for his event."

Of course, sacrificing family life is not an option for everyone – nor is it a necessity. But reaching our full potential requires a redistribution of energy, and this will usually come at the expense of another part of our lives – at least temporarily.

We start selecting our foundations when we choose the environment that surrounds us and recognise the triggers and barriers that stand in the way of our success.

We always ask our clients: "How is it going to feel tomorrow if you don't do this today?"

Let's say, if your family life is a priority for you yet you choose to spend every weekday evening at the gym or at the pub, you are going to wake up each morning feeling distanced from your partner and kids, as you swap stories on how you each spent the previous evening, instead of joking about your shared experiences. While it may be easy to justify this time away from home, if your family time is more important than your social life or your fitness regime, then clearly your energy is not being distributed in the best possible way.

We are all guilty of victimising ourselves as a way of justifying poor choices and this victim complex takes root as soon as we allow ourselves to entertain self-limiting beliefs.

This is an issue that David has come up against many times in his career, when it was easier to give in and admit exhaustion or frustration, rather than fighting past those instincts.

"It was a Wednesday morning, it was a recovery session and the recovery session was 4,000m straight," he says. "I just had to dive in and swim for 4,000m and then get out again.

"I was halfway through the week, it was proper hump day, by then I'd probably already done close to 30,000m in the pool, plus two gym sessions and a yoga session, and the thought of diving in and doing 4,000m was the last thing I wanted to do.

"I would dive in and with each and every stroke I'd be thinking, 'I do not want to be here. This is not helping me. I am anything but recovered right now.' And guess what? I came out and felt absolutely miserable and hated every moment of it.

"But gradually I learnt to love that session and the process, for me, was being able to see it as an opportunity to practice some stuff. There were some technique issues that I needed to improve, so I thought, 'I might as well use this session, at least to address some of the technique things.' My left hand was coming out slightly further than it ought to have done, so I wasn't getting my optimum pull, so I was going to change that.

"All of a sudden I started to find benefit in that session. Then I started to do this body scan - for three strokes I would focus on one part of my body and then I would move onto the next one. So it might start with my left index fingertip. I would focus on that for three strokes and go, 'Where's that? How does that feel? That's good,' or make a small correction.

"Then I would move onto my wrist, onto my elbow, onto the outside of my left shoulder, to my nose, to my chin, to whatever else. And it was amazing how quickly that session then went. It was just remarkable because I was so in the moment, I was so aware of what I was doing; I totally saw the benefit in it. Every other session was two and a half hours, that session was an hour, and all of a sudden it was a total reward, it was the session I looked forward to more than any other because I saw that direct connection to where I wanted to get to."

By rejecting his negative thinking, David was able to

energise his least-favourite training session and use it to improve his performance in an unexpected way.

REFERENCES

(1) Klein, Gary. (2007). Performing a Project Pre-mortem. Harvard Business Review. September 2007 Issue. Available at: https://hbr.org/2007/09/performing-a-project-premortem. [viewed June 2019].

(2) Huffington, Arianna. (2014). Thrive: The Third Metric to Redefining Success and Creating a Happier Life. London: Ebury Press

(3) Schwartz, Tony and McCarthy, Catherine. (2007). Manage Your Energy, Not Your Time. Harvard Business Review. October 2007 Issue. Available at: https://hbr.org/2007/10/manage-your-energy-not-your-time. [viewed June 2019].

(4) Mitchell, Deborah J, Russo, J. Edward, Pennington, Nancy. (1989). Back to the Future: Temporal perspective in the explanation of events. Journal of Behavioral Decision Making. January 1989 Issue. Available at: https://www.researchgate.net/publication/227768493_Back_to_the_future_Temporal_perspective_in_the_explanation_of_events. [viewed June 2019].

3.4 HOW TO APPLY

Setting and maintaining our foundations requires a commitment to optimising our energy reserves and learning from our mistakes. When we are trying to optimise our energy reserves, it is important to understand what is dragging on our ability to reach our wins, and what is propelling us forward.

A useful exercise is to take a stack of sticky notes and a pen and think about how your energy is divided.

Set a timer for two minutes and list as many things as possible, allocating one sticky note for each activity. Then group the sticky notes into themes – these may include work, family life, social life, hobbies, and personal growth. Then calculate the percentage of energy that is spent on each of these themes.

This will give us an overview of where we are spending our energy in our lives at the present time, but it may not represent our ideal energy split. What percentage are you spending on these different areas now? And what would you like those percentages to be?

Exercise: Present and future energy split

Where my time is spent	% (current)	% (future)

There will always be a few areas which we take for granted – many of us never prioritise self care, for instance, even though it is a hugely important foundation, regardless of the win that we are working towards. If we are currently only spending about 2% of our time on self care, maybe we could increase that to 5%? Once we have made that decision, we must ensure that we are actually using that 5% on self care and only self care – and not sacrificing that time elsewhere. This may mean spending 15 minutes a day practicing yoga, meditation or turning off your phone and reading a book for an hour once a week.

Family and friends time also tends to be overlooked when we are focusing on our end win, but this support system is incredibly important and could make the difference between success and failure. We all need to have people around us who can encourage us to keep going when we meet new obstacles, and to cheer us on when we reach new milestones.

However, it is not enough to simply base our time on where we are in our lives right now. We need to make room for those ratios to shift slightly as our focus changes. For instance, the decision to deprioritise family may accelerate that path to the win, but it could also cause major issues in the future when that win has changed from 'being promoted at work' to 'spending more time with family after retirement'. By sacrificing family time now, you may find it harder to prioritise it in the future.

It is important to understand that our wins and our priorities will change over time. Think about the person you want to be in a year, ten years, or 20 years' time. Do the same exercise. If you were able to design your life, how would you be spending your time and energy at that fixed point in the future?

Maybe our family time was at 20% before we did the exercise, but we reduced it to 10% in order to meet our other commitments. It may be that we need to make up for lost time by increasing our family time to 30% after our win has been achieved.

Once we can identify and articulate these different themes, we can take a critical look at where we are now, and where we want to be, and identify the gaps. This exercise will quickly reveal the changes that are required in order to be the person we want to be.

It is then up to us to close any gaps in our energy distribution, and to maximise the time that we spend in each area. For instance, we could potentially free up an extra hour in the day by avoiding social media during working hours, or by switching off our phone notifications for several hours at a time to a minimise distractions.

Of course, it's unrealistic to believe that these changes can happen all at once, but by setting out your ratios, you can start to make some meaningful changes.

Start with the environment that we inhabit. For instance, if a long and unreliable commute is acting as a drag, look at alternative modes of transport. Perhaps you could start by walking or cycling to work once a week.

If work or social stresses are having a negative effect on your free time, make a commitment to turn off your phone and laptop at 9pm each night.

Encourage your family, friends and colleagues to support you by keeping them in the loop. This has the added benefit of reinforcing your commitment to change, as you have made a public declaration that you will feel bound to stick to.

Each of these steps brings us closer to owning our identity because we are actively choosing to spend our time and energy on only those things that are furthering our goals. By claiming ownership of our own identity, our guiding principles and values, and the way we choose to spend our time and energy – we become stronger and more confident in our goals and ambitions.

People are in much more control than they think they are. We have a lot more decision-making rights than we may realise. We have an incredibly high ability to recharge and increase our capacity, to be able to select where we spend our energy, how quickly we are able to recharge our energy, and what it is that actually gives us that energy to begin with.

The challenge is to accept this as a fact and start laying the foundations for a productive and energetic future.

One way to do this is by mapping out your time to ensuring that you honour your chosen foundations. The time/energy diagram (figure 3.1) shows how to map a day against your energy and time. In this exercise map the key moments in your day that require your optimal performance and consider how you will prepare, recover and adapt from each, to best manage your energy.

Exercise: Map your energy and time

Energy and Time

Energy generating activities

Energy depleting activites

Performance enhancement activities

As well as pre-empting energy generating and depleting activities you can challenge yourself to see how you can convert activities from drain to gain. For example, commuting in rush hour on the bus could be energy draining. But a slight improvement could be listening to your favourite podcast or audiobook. A significant gain could involve swapping the bus for a bike, enabling you to address you exercise element at the same time.

Download the workbook for this chapter at: *WhatDoesItTakeToWin.com/workbook*

3.5 SUMMARY

The most important thing that we can take from this chapter is the realisation that we choose our own foundations. We are not victims of our surroundings or our circumstances – we can make a conscious effort to prioritise those areas which are important to us, and minimise the time and energy that we spend on everything else. By doing this, we can remain true to ourselves and give ourselves the best possible chance of happiness and fulfilment in life, at work and at the highest levels of the sporting world.

Strong foundations build confidence. They provide a blueprint that we can refer to any time we feel like we are not making progress. Our foundations remind us who we are and what is truly important to us, and this forces us to manage our energy in a positive way, eliminating drag and propelling ourselves forward so that we can reach our goals in life.

Our energy reserves are limited, so we owe it to ourselves to spend these reserves wisely. That may mean making some hard decisions – like the professional cyclist who had to sacrifice family time. But as long as our foundations are strong and truly reflective of our values and identity, we can always turn to them for guidance on how to make the most of our time and energy.

Chapter 4

Time travel to your win
– what would be amazing?

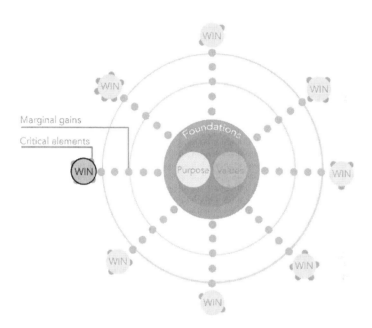

4.1 INTRODUCING CLARITY OF THE WIN...

With our foundations in place, we can start focusing on the win. Our win exists beyond the nucleus of our atomic confidence. But just like the electrons that buzz around the nucleus of an atom, our win can sometimes feel like it is just beyond our grasp. It flickers in and out of sight even as our core purpose, identity and foundations remain the same. This is why is it so important to take some time to work on the clarity of our win – to see it and understand it so that we never lose our focus, even when the win seems distant.

The clarity of the win can easily be confused with the idea of purpose. But while our purpose is all about our ultimate impact on our community, driven by our passion, the clarity of the win represents an actual outcome. Purpose lies at our core, acting as an internal compass, the win on the other hand is a moment in time providing us with evidence that we are on track. The win is a tangible representation of our purpose, in the same way a behaviour that is not representative of our values demonstrates an inauthentic person; a win that is not congruent to our purpose is a distraction and will be ultimately unfulfilling.

With a win, there has to be absolute clarity around what we want to achieve – we should be able to feel it, see it, smell it, hear it, and touch it. The clearer we make it, the more obvious the choices to achieve the win becomes.

If we are to give ourselves the best chance of success, we have to place ourselves in the future and ask – what would be amazing? From there, we work backwards to piece together the path to that amazing moment, and to eliminate as many of the barriers and risks as we can along the way.

Without clarity of the win, we can end up on the wrong path, chasing glory in the wrong places, and missing out on the moments of joy and success that we experience along the way. An unclear 'win' can lead to disappointment and failure, as David Carry discovered at the peak of his career.

"When we were training for the 2008 Beijing Olympics, it was the culmination of four years of getting up at five in the morning and swimming 70km a week, missing Christ-mases, weddings, birthdays, all in service of winning that medal," David says.

"I genuinely thought that it was my purpose in life to win an Olympic medal and that's what we were aiming for.

"We got through the heats and we qualified in fourth place, but we knew that we had a lot still in the tank. We had a game plan that we were ready to perform and during the final, each member of the relay team really stepped up and performed incredibly. I got a personal best – I actually beat my target time.

"Unfortunately, so did four other teams. We missed the medal by just 0.8 seconds. That was something that we had not even considered – that our best may not be 'the' best. And that was one thing that was completely out of our control. We may not have won the medal, but we certainly achieved our 'win'."

This is a great example of the dangers of being unpre-pared for the reality of the win. David had not considered one crucial element - that his team would not be faster than the teams from the US, China and Russia. But that doesn't take anything away from the fact that both David and his relay team achieved their own fastest ever times during that race.

This is the difference between a win and a purpose. While both are important steps on our journey to success, only the 'win' is guaranteed to reward hard work. And the more clarity we have around that win, the clearer the choices to achieving it.

It is worth remembering that it is also possible to have more than one win on the horizon at any given time, with each win associated with a different foundation. In fact, by setting multiple wins, we actually increase our chances of achieving a fulfilled life.

However, one of these wins will always be more significant than the others, and this is where it becomes important to establish our priorities.

To illustrate, a restaurant owner may consider her main

'win' to be the ability to run a profitable business. But she may also aim to win a nationally-recognised award, to get great reviews, and to build up a loyal customer base. In her personal life, her ultimate win may be to create a kitchen garden full of organic herbs and produce.

All of these wins can run concurrently, as long as the focus is on the most important win of all – turning a profit.

The restaurant may experience financial ups and downs along the way to profitability, but along the way these other wins, the awards, the happy customers, the growth of the garden and the good reviews – will help her to stay focused and engaged, and they will give her the confidence to keep pursuing success.

4.2 DEFINING

In order to achieve the clarity of the win, we have to do a bit of time travelling. Imagine yourself in 20 years' time, what sort of a person are you? What do other people think of you? What has your greatest accomplishment been?

Perhaps you see yourself as a renowned professor with a string of academic awards and doctorates behind you. Maybe you are living in rural bliss, surrounded by animals and famous for your organic farm shop. Or maybe you are taking early retirement after a lifetime of hard work, so you can finally spend some quality time with your family and friends. Whatever you are picturing in your ideal future, if it makes you happy, that's your win.

The 'win' itself is a future-bound, compelling and tangible statement of intent that has a clear achievement, measure and timeframe. It is representative of what we would like the outcome of our effort to be.

It is also amazing. It is the moment that we have built towards our whole life, and it is an opportunity to show the world exactly what we are capable of.

The win is the finish line at the end of a long race

– we might be standing at the starting blocks right now, but we know exactly where we are going, and we know that we will get there eventually, as long as we follow our path.

The path to win

But how do we get there?

In an ideal world, there would be a straight line between where we are and the things we want to achieve. And in a simple world with no external influences, that can be achieved. Say your aim is to finish this book in one sitting – that's doable! All you have to do is to keep reading until you're done. But as soon as we start adding complexity, the difficulty increases at an exponential rate. So your reading time is interrupted by the school run, by work, a training session, or simply by the basic need to sleep and eat. These interruptions can make even a modest task seem complicated and less attainable.

In fact, this linear way of planning can even become counterproductive. When we think we are following a straight line towards our wins, we become frustrated when we encounter a few bends along the way. This can cause us stress and anguish, and that can lead to failure.

We give ourselves a much better chance of success if

we can anticipate the bends and adapt our path accordingly. We are not trying to predict the future – we are trying to identify an aspiration and then arm ourselves with the best possible choices and the ability to react and interact with the world around us, in order to give ourselves the best chance of success.

This requires an ability to learn from the past; to identify the highest-impact risks and the likelihood of these risks getting in the way of our success. As we learned when we conducted our pre-mortem: if a problem can be predicted, so too can the solution.

Overcoming fear

The most common obstacle to success is fear. This is often an unconscious reaction that tells us we can't do the things we want to do. What if we mess up? What if we fail? What if we look foolish just by trying to achieve our wins?

Fear can be absolutely paralysing for performance. At Track Record, we call it 'future catastrophising', where we take a fact or a belief and assume the worst about it. But channelled correctly, this can actually be turned into a positive. By imagining the worst possible outcomes in a series of likely scenarios, we can put in place a plan to avoid or manage them. This lesson is just as useful in sport and business as it is in life itself.

When David Carry discovered the benefits of future catastrophising, he was nowhere near a pool.

"When my wife was pregnant with our first child, we were going to all these antenatal classes," says David. "And part of these classes involved talking through all the problems and the issues that might happen to our baby, and how to handle them.

"We weren't immediately sure if we wanted to go, it all sounded quite morbid and stressful, but in hindsight, I'm so glad we did.

"We were given a lot of really valuable information about how to minimise the risk of your child coming to harm. For instance, what kind of stair gates to get; what kind of plugs to put in your wall to minimise the risk of electrocution; not leaving hot pans on the stove; and what to do if your child is choking.

"To stop a child choking you have to hit them in the right way to be able to dislodge the item. We practised this procedure and I realised just quite how hard you can hit a child without hurting them. It was shocking.

"Flash forward to four months later, and I'm looking after my daughter Josephine. She swallowed something and couldn't dislodge it and she started choking. This went on for about 30 seconds – it was just awful.

"I swung into action, flipped her around and hit her on her back several times and eventually this thing dislodged.

"Had I not faced my fear and gone to that antenatal class, I would have had no idea what to do at that moment. I would have just frozen. But because we had planned for these worst-case scenarios, I was able to pre-load a solution into my brain and put it into action when it mattered most."

This shows us the value of preparing for the worst, even when the worst-case scenario seems too awful to consider. By allowing himself to imagine the horror of watching his child choke, David was able to plan for disaster and learn a skill that ultimately saved his daughter's life.

This goes back to the core principle of confidence, which we covered in chapter 2 – control. What is within our control? And how can we use that knowledge to plan ahead? By visualising our future warts and all, we can take control of our own narrative, and ensure that our path to success is as clear as it can possibly be. This will inspire confidence in ourselves and in the possibility of achieving that win. When we are more self-assured, we are more likely to be able to deliver our best performance. And when we can deliver our best performance, we increase our chances of success.

The power of the win

The win itself is a powerful motivating tool. It dictates our direction of travel and helps us to shape how we are going to get there. When we don't know with certainty what we are trying to achieve, we can't figure out how we're going to do it. By naming the win, we are committing to that journey with confidence, and giving ourselves permission to celebrate.

So, what are the key components of a win?

1. It should be challenging enough that it feels inspirational but not unobtainable.

For instance, if our aim is to get fitter, we may decide that our win will come when we complete a full marathon in less than four hours. This is the type of win that is achievable, but only if we are prepared to put a lot of work in. It may take several years of training to reach that point, but it is possible.

Alternatively, if our fitness goal is to climb Mt Everest, the odds are very much stacked against us, and there is a multitude of uncontrollable issues that could get in the way of that win.

2. It should be something that can be measured

The win should be a tangible thing, a moment in time or a known achievement. It should be very clear what the outcome is going to look like, so we need to be able to define what success is for that win. What will it feel like? What will it look like? How will we know that we are achieving that win?

For most students, the 'win' is the graduation ceremony, when they are handed the certification of their academic achievement at a formal ceremony. This type of win is easy to imagine, as it has been achieved by many others before us – but that doesn't mean it will be any easier for us to achieve. It simply makes the path to that win even clearer.

3. It should provide evidence of its existence

An effective win should contain an achievement of some kind so that we can look back on it and remember how far we have come. That evidence may take the form of a trophy or a medal; a certificate; or even just a photo. Without evidence, it is harder to visualise the win in its entirety, and that will make the journey to success just that little bit harder to see.

4. It should be a multi-sensory experience

When we talk about 'the clarity of the win', we are not simply talking about visual representation. It is a multi-sensory experience – we should be able to describe it, to talk about how it will feel when we have achieved it. Then we need to determine the critical elements that have to be in place for that win to become true.

5. It should involve some stakeholders

We all need a little support sometimes, and our support networks can be an invaluable lifeline on our journey towards the win. By involving a few key people, we create stakeholders in our win. They will be invested enough to offer encouragement, and skilled enough to provide us with advice and identify our blind spots.

But the most important quality that our stakeholders must have is the ability to care, really care, about what we are trying to achieve. This may require us to make an emotional connection with a coach, manager or financial backer. Instead of saying: 'I need you to time my run', we could say 'I'm a bit worried that my sprints aren't fast enough – could you help me identify any weaknesses so that I can achieve my dream of playing professional football?'. The same question is being asked but in a more emotional way. The stakeholder doesn't need to care about you personally, but they do need to share in that 'clarity of the win' in order to throw their support behind the task at hand.

We must have complete clarity around our vision of

the win, and we must surround ourselves with all the tools, problem-solving abilities and stakeholders that we can find.

The more clarity we have, the more likely we are to achieve it. So the more we can articulate to ourselves and to others what that looks like, the more we are then able to break it down, to control the controllables and deliver the performance.

4.3 SCIENCE AND EVIDENCE

"When someone becomes disconnected from the future and their contribution to it, they underperform"
Brendon Burchard

Visualisation is a tried and tested method for helping us to get to our win. And the more specific we can be about how that 'win' looks and feels, the higher the chances that we will get there.

In 2002, professors Edwin A. Locke and Gary P. Latham (2) completed a 25-year study on goal-setting, which included more than 400 laboratory tests. They concluded that: "specific, high (hard) goals lead to a higher level of task performance than do easy goals or vague, abstract goals such as the exhortation to 'do one's best'.

"So long as a person is committed to the goal, has the requisite ability to attain it, and does not have conflicting goals, there is a positive, linear relationship between goal difficulty and task performance. Because goals refer to future valued outcomes, the setting of goals is first and foremost a discrepancy-creating process. It implies discontent with one's present condition and the desire to attain an object or outcome."

Their research explains that setting specific goals consistently leads to a higher performance than just urging people to do their best.

When we are confident in our ability to set our wins, train and manage adversity, then the path to that 'win' becomes much clearer. We can actually see a future where we succeed. From there, it is just a matter of working backwards.

David Carry experienced this in the run-up to the London 2012 Olympics.

"In order to deliver my best performance in the London 2012 Olympics, I had to, first of all, imagine myself there and think about what I might need at that moment in order to be totally confident standing on that diving block, ready to deliver my best performance," he says.

"I had to put myself in that arena and imagine what it would be like. What worries might I have? What would I wish I had done more of or less of? Then I had to think about what I could realistically do between now and then to increase my chances of feeling confident about my ability to perform.

"I began every training session like this. I would ask myself: 'In order for me to get to that moment in London 2012, what do I need to do today?'

"There was a direct connection between what I was doing and what I was going to be doing and so the choices I was making in training would contribute to helping me achieve my ultimate 'win'.

"In the end, I ended up giving my best ever performance at London 2012.

"At the age of 30, I was able to beat my own personal best time, and I reached the Olympic final. It was the closest I ever got to my potential."

Of course, David did not simply wish his 'win' into existence. During those training sessions, he thought about all the potential obstacles that could get in the way of his Olympic dream. For instance, he knew that he was at a greater risk of getting a back injury, so he mapped out a treatment plan that would help his recovery as quickly as possible. When this injury eventually did occur, just three weeks before the 2012 Olympic trials – he didn't panic. Instead, he reverted to his treatment plan and he was fit and healthy again in time for his first race.

Trying to understand that critical pathway is the key to helping us avoid failure and a loss of confidence.

Professor Steve Peters would probably say that David's reaction to his injury was a triumph of his 'human' sensibility over his 'inner chimp'. In The Chimp Paradox (3), Prof Peters tells us that we essentially have two brains – the frontal (human) and the limbic (chimp). Our chimp brain is an "emotional machine" that we must learn to control if we want to behave calmly and rationally, with a clear goal in mind.

There will be many moments on our path to the win where we will be at risk of emotional overload. David could have easily turned his injury into a career-ending catastrophe – he could have reacted emotionally, not practically, and deprived himself of the opportunity to recover in time for the Olympics. Instead, because he had complete clarity of his win, he was able to stay focused and rely on his prior planning to get him back on track.

"Psychological evidence says that we need to dream big and set extremely challenging goals if we want to increase our chances of success," Prof. Peters says.

"Don't aim for the moon but the stars. The 'moon' is a goal that you know you can achieve by effort. The 'stars' are a goal that you could achieve by great effort and it will feel fantastic to reach the goal. If you aim for the moon then your inner chimp can get complacent; but if you aim higher for the stars your chimp and human commit to it and get excited by the big challenge. Therefore make sure your dreams excite you, as you are more likely to achieve them and if you do miss the stars you might still reach the moon!"

In The 7 Habits of Highly Effective People (4), Habit 2 tells us to "begin with the end in mind". The author and philosopher Stephen Covey believed that by having a clear goal in mind, we give ourselves a much better chance of actually achieving it.

This concept has been described again and again by scientists, academics, philosophers and self-help gurus.

Visualising success inspires success and gives us the best possible odds of reaching our win. This is true whether we are setting individual wins or working as a group.

When there is a clear achievement on the horizon; when we can smell it, feel it and describe it in fine detail – then we simply have to keep it in sight and we will get there eventually.

REFERENCES

(1) Edwin A. Locke and Gary P. Latham. (2006). New Directions in Goal Setting. Current Directions in Psychological Science. Vol. 15, Issue 5. [cited June 2019]. Available from: https://journals.sagepub.com/doi/abs/10.1111/j.1467-8721.2006.00449.x

(2) Peters, S. (2012) The Chimp Paradox. Croydon: Vermilion. P.3-4.

(3) Covey, S. (1989) The 7 Habits of Highly Effective People. London: Simon & Schuster. P.95

4.4 HOW TO APPLY

Once we know what our win – or wins – will feel like, we can interrogate all of the things that are critical in order for us to get there. These things may be psychological or physical. They might involve creating new habits or breaking old ones, or they may simply be a matter of training.

For instance, say we have a goal to lose weight, what is standing in the way of this dream becoming a reality? What problems do we foresee?

In this example, a cupboard full of crisps and chocolate may represent a potential obstacle to our win. But this is something we can control. All we have to do is get rid of the junk food and replace it with healthier snacks.

Another barrier to weight loss might be a lack of free time for exercise. We can control this to a certain extent by getting up a little earlier, or eating at our desk so we can go to the gym at lunchtime. But there will always be unforeseen events that get in the way of our workout routine – a sick child, an urgent meeting or even an injury that we have sustained. We may not be able to prevent these things from happening, but we can come up with a few alternative scenarios, such as a home-based workout, or a dietary amendment that makes up for a lack of activity.

Now let's apply this same theory to our own wins.

In the last chapter, we selected our foundations, and now it is time to leverage these foundations to set a clear win.

STEP ONE - Select a foundation
How far into the future can you see in relation to this foundation? For instance, if your foundation is health and fitness, how far do you think you can pursue this? Do you want muscle mass? Could you focus on this to such an extent that you are able to enter bodybuilding compe-

titions? Do you see yourself winning those contests? Remember, you have chosen your foundations, so you are already off to a great start, don't be afraid to think big when it comes to the win.

Exercise: My foundation

My foundation	Visualising the detail

STEP TWO – Describe your win

Now, imagine yourself in the moment of the win. What does it feel like? Who is there? What do you hear and what do you smell? Where are you? By conjuring up this image in as much detail as possible you can imagine a world where your win is your reality. How does that make you feel?

Exercise: My win

My win	What it feels like

STEP THREE – Write your statement of intent

This is your path to success. Make sure you consider a few key points:

- The achievement itself – what does your win look like?
- The measurement – how will you know that you have been successful?
- The timeline – by which date will you have achieved your win?

Exercise: Timeline to success

TIMELINE TO SUCCESS

STEP FOUR – Repeat with the other foundations.

By following these steps, you will gain the clarity that you need to achieve your win, time and time again. With each win, you will become more confident in your abilities, and this will encourage you to press ahead and chase even bigger ambitions until you are truly living at your best.

Download the workbook for this chapter at: *WhatDoesItTakeToWin.com/workbook*

4.5 SUMMARY

Winning is not everything, but 'the win' certainly is. When we identify a tangible win in our lives, we are making good on our sense of purpose and our values. And by setting multiple wins, we are showing respect for our various foundations by allowing them to become the basis of our success. In this way, we can optimise our existing talents and passions in the most positive way possible.

But it all comes down to clarity. A vague notion of a win is not going to be enough to get us there. David Carry didn't simply dream of becoming a better swimmer, he dreamed of Olympic glory. By imagining himself on the podium before a race, he was able to motivate himself to train more efficiently for the specific purpose of winning a medal for his country. When he missed out on a medal by mere milliseconds, he was able to see that his win was not the medal, it was the ability to push himself to be the best that he could possibly be by logging his best-ever time in the 2008 Beijing Olympics.

When the win is clear, we can work backwards to identify all the obstacles and risks that stand between us and success. We can troubleshoot all the foreseeable problems until we have come up with a series of solutions. When we can imagine a worst-case scenario and plan for a workaround, suddenly it doesn't feel like such a worst-case scenario after all.

Of course, there will always be some uncontrollable risks that we can't predict. But by clearing the path of the problems that are within our control, we are able to free up the energy to handle these unpredictable events – after all, they should be the only real problems that we encounter.

The clarity of the win gives us a prototype for success so that all we have to do is stay the course until we reach that amazing moment.

Chapter 5

Design your critical elements
– What has to be true
to achieve the win?

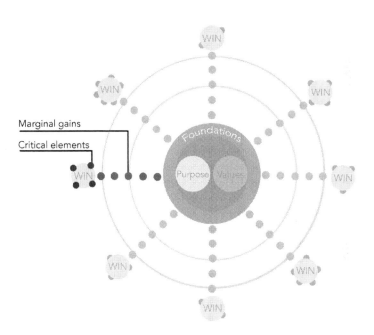

5.1 INTRODUCING CRITICAL ELEMENTS

We know what our win looks like and feels like, so now

we need to examine all the critical elements that have to be in place before that win is possible. What needs to happen in order for us to reach our win? And what key factors will make it impossible to get there?

Critical elements live in the future. They are the breakdown of the win into chunks, with each chunk representing something that must come true in order for our win to be achieved. If we were to take away one of these critical elements, the win would not be possible.

At this stage of our confidence journey, we need to rely on the strength of our atomic core to propel ourselves forward towards our win. This will involve an honest interrogation of our fears so that we can prepare ourselves with the best possible choices and the ability to react and interact with the world around us.

By doing this, we can effectively troubleshoot our path to the win, by anticipating any problems or delays before they occur and have a plan in place to deal with them. This part of the process is about being able to gather information quickly, spot the patterns and the experiences that we have had in the past and the lessons that we have learned, and then figure out what works and what does not.

That constant environment of change mirrors the reality of life. The world never stops changing. We can begin our journey to success in one environment but end it in a completely different one. For instance, a planned trip around the world may be changed by new visa restrictions; or a carefully-managed five-year career plan may be accelerated due to an unexpected job opportunity. We must adapt to these new circumstances without losing sight of our win.

Say that win was to become a partner at your firm – the critical elements to success would involve:

1. A track record of success
2. A proven ability that you possess the skills and knowledge to perform the role
3. The required attitude and behaviours

4. The ability to inspire through the clarity of your vision.

But just as a partnership appears to be inevitable, the firm is acquired by a much larger company. This is an uncontrollable event that threatens to stand in the way of our win, or perhaps presents opportunities for even faster promotion. So, it does not spell disaster. Company acquisitions happen all the time and this is a situation that could have been anticipated several years in advance.

By interrogating the critical elements of this win, we would have been able to identify the gap analysis of where you are today and where you need to be in order for your win to be true. The planning phase in Chapter 6 will help you to see how to bridge this gap, and through this planning, we can protect the possibility of the win.

We also need to be able to make our win as attainable as possible by breaking each critical element down into a series of marginal gains, which will keep us motivated and focused no matter what. For instance, if our aim is to complete a 10k race, then our critical elements will include fitness, nutrition, hydration and recovery. If we don't look after each of these things, we won't be able to complete the 10k.

We then need to be able to prioritise these elements, so that we know where we are going to place our energy right from the outset. And then we need to go even deeper, identifying the many marginal gains that go into each element, each one bringing us a little closer to our 'win'.

This process can be surprisingly painful for many people, as it forces us to dig into the minutiae of our pre-win routine and to confront some difficult truths. Where fitness is a critical element; the risk of injury may represent a big potential problem. Where teamwork is a critical element; we may need to change our style of communication.

And then there are the uncontrollable factors which can get between us and our win. These are unpredictable and can be potentially devastating, but we can do our best to prepare ourselves by anticipating all types of problems – from the 'knowns' to the 'unknowns'.

When we take the time to do this in the planning stage, we can spare ourselves from any unexpected distractions and interruptions further down the line. By being aware of the challenges ahead of us, we can create a more realistic path to our win, and hugely increase our chances of getting there in the end.

5.2 DEFINING

A critical element is a fact, not an opinion. It should be a proven entity – something that will definitely help us to reach our win if it is in place, but without which we will definitely fail. For instance, if we want to plan a two-week road trip along the coast of California, one thing we will definitely need is a passport. Without a passport, international travel will be impossible. With a passport, the trip is possible. It is not the only element that needs to be in place to make that trip happen, but it is certainly a critical one.

Our critical elements are crucial to the win, so we need to be prepared to fully unpack each one and be truly honest with ourselves about where we are falling short. Is our perception of our abilities true? Are our critical elements actually in place?

These critical elements are important because they are offering us an opportunity to control the determinants of our success rather than just hoping for an outcome. We are figuring out what we can actually control in order to improve our chances of achieving that win.

Once we understand which critical elements we actually need, it's just a matter of creating clarity around what is required to fulfil these elements. For instance, we may need to break them down into a series of timeframes or marginal gains. So if our win as mentioned in Chapter 4, is to lose weight and one of our critical elements is nutrition, we may start by taking all the crisps and chocolate out of the house and replacing it with healthy snacks. We may then download a nutrition-tracking app and start inputting our meals. We can then check in with this app on a regular basis to make sure we are still on track to meet our weight-loss goals.

By breaking down the critical element of nutrition, we can create a few mini wins for ourselves along the way, and use them to keep us motivated.

This is how Hannah MacLeod prepared herself for the field hockey pool games at the 2016 Olympics in Rio de Janeiro. The first match was against Australia, and the 'win' was to get each team member to be able to think, feel and ultimately behave like a world-class team.

They started by identifying the critical elements that surrounded each individual's ability to do those things in that moment.

"That involved a certain level of fitness," says Hannah. "We needed to be able to perform repeated bouts of high-intensity work, that was essential. We needed players who were able to problem solve in a very complex environment, which seems like quite a broad requirement, but actually dictated our training environment so that we could develop problem solvers and a problem-solving attitude within the team.

"We also needed athletes to be able to communicate effectively, even when we were in front of a massive crowd that is drowning out our voices. So what might non-verbal communication look like from the side of the pitch?

"In the changing room, a coach has only two minutes to deliver a message, so we needed to look at that moment and ensure that we can absorb that message as players and have that absolute clarity and understanding before we go back out again and deliver.

"It was incredible for me, as an individual within a

team, to experience the level of confidence that comes with identifying these crucial components and working towards them together."

"Once you know what is required of you, all you can do is to stay focused and work bloody hard to do it. And when you are seeing that same confidence and commitment from all the people around you as well, how can you ever think that if you lose that match you've failed? The win is in the execution."

Incidentally, Team GB beat Team Australia 2-1.

Hannah's experience at the 2016 Olympics underlines the importance of critical elements in preparing for a win. When we are in this planning stage, our critical elements can help keep us concentrated on the moment of the win. They can also help us to save a huge amount of time by foreseeing any problems and dealing with them ahead of time.

Discovering your critical elements

"There are known knowns; there are things we know we know. We also know there are known unknowns; that is to say we know there are some things we do not know. But there are also unknown unknowns — the ones we don't know we don't know." – Donald Rumsfeld.

Former US defence secretary Donald Rumsfeld was roundly ridiculed when he made this famous statement about the existence – or lack thereof - of weapons of mass destruction in Iraq in 2002. But his words have gone on to be quoted by academics and scientists (1) as a way of describing unexpected outcomes which had not been taken into consideration at the beginning of a particular project. We can apply this philosophy to our own critical elements by accepting that there will always be a few uncontrollable factors that may interfere with our plans and threaten our win.

So if our win is to become a doctor and we know that one of the critical elements for success is getting a medical degree, then we need to firstly examine the known risks. For instance, what if we fail some of our exams? Could we retake them? How would this impact on our timeline? Will we have to make an alteration to our plan?

Now think about a few unknowns – a bereavement, a health issue, an unexpected relocation. It doesn't really matter what sort of 'unknown' we use as an example because unknowns are, by their nature, unpredictable. But by thinking about them from the outset, we are at least acknowledging the existence of outside forces and we can mentally prepare ourselves for outlying events. We may have to take an unscheduled break from our exercise regime or to revisit our plans to account for a changing environment.

We need to interrogate the risks – do we actually have time to do this? Can we access those resources that we need? Do we have enough passion to get us to the finish line? Are we prepared to make certain sacrifices along the way?

This is going to require a real honesty of self. We need to be able to probe the knowns and unknowns right at the beginning of the planning stage because then we have more time to understand what the unknowns really are, and how we can protect ourselves from them.

We can prioritise those unknowns in terms of what we can feasibly understand in the time that is available to us, and we can then set out to understand as many of them as possible during the planning phase. This helps us to create some certainty in our environment so we can make the right decisions and learn as much as we can along the way. By simply acknowledging the 'unknown unknowns', we can at least minimise their effect on our critical elements.

Marginal gains

Our marginal gains are the little wins that help to move us forward towards our end win. Each marginal win should correspond with one of our critical elements and they should be listed in order of priority so that we can use our time as efficiently as possible. In isolation, each of these marginal gains may seem to represent the tiniest measure of progress. But step by step, gain by gain, they can lead us to the most ambitious of wins.

Each small step brings us closer to our biggest win

We start the process of examining our critical elements by creating a long list of things that we know, based on the questions we have asked, the research we have done, and the facts that we have. These things should automatically go on the long list.

Then there are going to be things that we don't know, where we need to do more research and ask more questions. We will probably have to prioritise these elements at some point in order to understand them.

We then make a big list of 'marginal gains', which are all the things, large and small, that will add up to a win, as shown in the table:

COMPLETING A 10K RACE. CRITICAL ELEMENT - TRAINING
MARGINAL GAINS IN ALPHABETICAL ORDER
Ensuring good hydration

COMPLETING A 10K RACE. CRITICAL ELEMENT - TRAINING
MARGINAL GAINS IN ALPHABETICAL ORDER
Finding a 10k race
Following other 10k runners on social media
Getting eight hours of sleep each night
Investing in good running shoe
Researching basic running techniques
Running at least three times a week
Signing up for the race
Speaking to other runners
Working on nutrition

If we looked at any single one of these marginal gains individually, they would probably appear random. But once we start to prioritise them into the key things that are going to make the biggest difference to our win, then we increase our chances of getting there in the end. An example of how this may look is in the next table:

COMPLETING A 10K RACE. CRITICAL ELEMENT - TRAINING
MARGINAL GAINS IN ORDER OF PRIORITY
Finding a 10k race
Signing up for the race
Working on nutrition
Getting eight hours of sleep each night
Ensuring good hydration
Researching basic running techniques
Running at least three times a week
Speaking to other runners
Investing in good running shoes
Following other 10k runners on social media

Each of these marginal gains is incredibly important in ensuring that we reach our win. If we identify all the small things and commit to them, they will add up to a big gain which is totally achievable.

We can also use these marginal gains as a motivating tool because we know that by doing each one of these things, we are directly contributing towards the critical element that will move us closer to our win. In chapter four, we learned how to conduct a pre-mortem to anticipate problems and understand how to manage them. This pre-mortem, combined with a focus on marginal gains, can make even the most ambitious win feel possible.

"Going into Rio 2016, my win was around actually delivering what was expected of me," explains Hannah. "I had a real clarity as to what my role was for the team; within that, what my strengths were; and therefore, what was absolutely within my control to deliver.

"For example, there was an expectation around my communication of the tactics that were being deployed by the opposition and therefore what we needed to do. There was an expectation that at the moment, under huge amounts of pressure and stress, in a packed stadium where you can't really hear anything, I would be able to deliver that information for the team. It was quite a small element, but it was a vital one. I had three years to effectively prepare for that moment. My win was to be the effective communicator of the team, to lead the team in tactical understanding.

"The win is completely wrapped up in a moment of time. There is a definite point. I can see the behaviour that I need to display and I have that endpoint in mind in terms of, now what is it that I need to be doing to enable me to do that in the future, which forms our critical elements." In Hannah's case, the critical elements on the pathway to that win included having really good relationships with her teammates.

"I had to understand how I needed to communicate to them because it is different for every single person," she says. "At the start of my journey, I had one style and that was it. That wasn't effective. I realised that my style of communication was within my control. So I chose to spend more time having one-on-one conversations with each teammate and learning how they prefer to communicate. Each one of these conversations moved me in the direction of my win."

In order to achieve her critical element of being a communicative team member, Hannah made a list of marginal gains that would help her reach that point, shown in the table:

CRITICAL ELEMENT – COMMUNICATION.
MARGINAL GAINS (IN ALPHABETICAL ORDER)
A thorough understanding of the team's tactics
Always including the subs
Having one-on-one conversations with each of the other 15 members of the team
Making eye contact while talking to players
Never shying away from a difficult conversation
Only say things that I believe

"Some of these marginal gains may seem superfluous," adds Hannah, "But – for instance – finding it easy to look someone in the eye while speaking to them? That shows respect and proves that we are listening to them, which develops the relationship. This then allows us to be able to bark orders on a pitch in a really loud stadium under extreme pressure."

Imagine that each of these marginal gains represents at least 1% of a critical element. Every single percentage is going to help us reach our win, and it is down to us whether we want to employ 67% or 99% or 100% of our marginal gains. How do we do this? By following the process.

5.3 SCIENCE AND EVIDENCE

"To execute strategy, leaders must set ambitious targets, translate them into specific metrics and milestones, make them transparent throughout the organisation, and discuss progress frequently." – Charles Sull and Donald Sull, authors of The Strategic Agility Project

One of the first things that we can do to help us on our path to the win is to identify someone else who has done it before, or at least done something similar. So, let's take that Californian road trip.

Perhaps a good place to start would be to read a book about someone else's road trip experience. If we know someone else who has done the trip in the past, we could invite them out for a coffee and ask them what we should prepare for. There is nothing wrong with asking for help, but this can be a tough task for a lot of people. We all like to think that we can do everything ourselves, but when we have a challenge in mind, we may need a lot more help than we think in order to get there.

If we set out to do something that someone we know has already tried to do, then they may be able to help us understand some of those critical elements that we had not considered. That's a part of planning that doesn't take a lot of time.

Luckily, there is no shortage of literature on the concepts of goal-setting and visualisation.

Anyone who has ever taken part in any type of performance management appraisal or training will probably be familiar with the concept of SMART objectives, but in their paper, The Strategic Agility Project (2), Charles and Donald Sull created a new acronym – FAST goals [The FAST model is © 2018 from MIT Sloan Management Review/Massachusetts Institute of Technology]. We can see how these two approaches differ in Figure 5.1

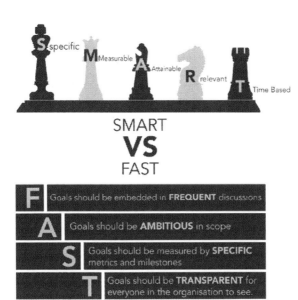

Figure 5.1. SMART vs FAST goals

SMART goals are defined as being Specific, Measurable, Attainable, Relevant and Time-based; while FAST goals should be Frequently discussed, Ambitious, Specific and Transparent.

Let's take an office relocation as an example. After ten years in a small, crowded office, the company needs to move to another location. The office move is going to require a lot organisation and planning if it is going to work.

Here's how we use SMART goals to achieve this.

Specific – do we know the exact location of the new office? Will it be accessible to all employees?

Measurable – what will a successful move look like? Will success mean minimising disruption in the workplace? Or can disruption be tolerated if it means more space for client meetings and new staff?

Attainable – can the company afford the new office space, and does the new office have all the amenities that are required?

Relevant – does the office move fit in with the company's growth plans? Will the move help to save money or expand the business?

Time-based – when does the move need to happen? Now, let's apply the FAST model.

Frequent discussion – is everyone at the firm aware of the move and the reasons behind it?

Ambitious – can the office move be used as an opportunity for growth?

Specific – is there a particular location that will help raise the company's profile?

Transparent - does every member of staff know what is required of them before, after and during the transition period?

While both models will produce the same end result – an office move - there is one major difference between these SMART and FAST goals. The SMART goals could feasibly be accomplished by one person acting as a project manager. By contrast, the FAST goals are much more inclusive and allow the company to treat the move as a way of consolidating the brand and its future.

The Sulls' research found that corporate targets were more likely to be met once the FAST principles had been applied. By discussing the critical elements of their projects at least once a quarter, corporate teams were more likely to stay on track and reach their wins. The more challenging and specific these wins were, the greater the likelihood that they would achieve them. And by promoting transparency across every part of the company, team members were motivated to do their best work and to keep each other on track as well.

Some of these elements have also been studied by Chakravarti et al, in a report titled Why You Should Stop Setting Easy Goals (3). Participants in the study were asked to choose between making modest improvements or maintaining the status quo, and the majority chose modest improvements.

"This finding held across all kinds of spheres — whether about achieving a higher grade point average (GPA), exercising more, completing more tasks, saving more, or working more hours," the report concluded. "Despite the fact that they knew these goals were harder, participants anticipated greater satisfaction from achieving modest positive changes as opposed to maintaining the status quo.

In his book, When, Daniel Pink (4), says that we have a habit of only taking our goals seriously once we are halfway through them. But if we plan properly and work towards that win right from the start, then we are more likely to achieve what we set out to achieve.

To be clear, a positive attitude won't guarantee success, but it will definitely increase the chances of success. We can avoid what Daniel Kahneman calls "delusional optimism" (5) by considering all the things that have to be taken into account in order to achieve what we set out to achieve. Therefore, proper planning aids decision-making and allows us to take control of the controllables.

This helps us to work out what resources we need in order to achieve our win - whether that's a support network, a training location, a university course, or access to finance. Identifying these resources makes it easier for us to commit to our wins, and helps us to avoid too many mistakes along the way.

By planning out these critical elements in advance, it also helps other people to understand what we need from them in order to achieve our win.

Delusional optimism happens when we just decide that we are going to achieve something, rather than actually sitting down and planning it out. When we are working towards an ambitious win, it is not enough to simply want to achieve it – we have to be able to put the work in too. This is a process of continually trying to do better and make better choices, and doing all we can to anticipate potential problems.

David Carry and his team experienced this in January 2012.

"We were coming into the final stages of the Olympic Games training and we were tracking really well," notes David. "I had just swum at the World Championships and had been happy with my results. I was looking forward to the next step going into London 2012. So everything was going well.

"I was at a training camp in the Spanish Sierra Nevada – we were one week into an incredibly intense four-week training programme when I discovered I had what turned out to be a bulging disc.

"This meant that the pads between my spine had become inflamed and were impinging on the nerves that run down either side of my back. It was a horrible pain running all the way down the right side of my body. And so it meant that I couldn't dive, I couldn't tumble turn, and I could barely walk when I bent over.

"That afternoon I was flown back to the UK and because of the team that I had, I was looked after incredibly well.

"I then had to go through three months of rehab, but I came out of it much faster and stronger, and a more resilient athlete, because about six months prior to that incident, we'd actually predicted it.

"We had gone through that process of identifying any risks and any fears that we had that were likely to get in our way. And because of the work that our physio had done, he identified that a key risk within me physically was my lower back. This had become an area of risk because we were dramatically increasing the number of dolphin kicks that I was doing under the water, and this can lead to a greater probability of inflammation, irritation and ultimately injury. So we discussed at length what would happen in the event of me having this situation.

"We decided that I would probably need to have some kind of anti-inflammation injection into my spine. I would then need to go through a period of building my core muscle to allow my spine to take the impact. Then I would have to see a chiropractor to realign my spine, and then I would have to work with the physio.

"To build you back up in terms of the patterning and it'll probably take about three months for you to get back on track again.

"The amazing thing was that usually, I would have had an emotional reaction as well as a physical one, but because we discussed it and even planned for it, I didn't have that emotional reaction.

"All those things that I'd feared actually did come true, but because I discussed it the fear disappeared and it became this automated process that we just kind of went through.

"So I flew back, had the surgery that I needed and went straight into working with my physio. Three months later, my first dive was at the Olympic trials to qualify for the London 2012 Olympics.

"That's how tightly the plan went. And thankfully it was a successful outcome."

By conducting a pre-mortem on his Olympic journey, David was able to avoid the trap of delusional optimism by confronting the very real risk of injury and working on a plan to deal with it. And because his recovery plan had been put together right at the start of his training programme, he was able to get the help he needed without jeopardising his dream of competing in the London 2012 Olympics.

REFERENCES

(1) Logan, David C. (2009) Known knowns, known unknowns, unknown unknowns and the propagation of scientific enquiry. Journal of Experimental Botany, Volume 60, Issue 3. [cited June 2019]; pages 712-714. Available from: https://academic.oup.com/jxb/article/60/3/712/453685

(2) Sull, Charles and Sull, Donald. (2018) With goals FAST beats SMART. MIT Sloan Management Review. [cited June 2019]. Available from: https://sloanreview.mit.edu/strategic-agility

(3) Chakravarti, D., Chattopadhyay, A., and Staatogiannakis, A. (2018) Why You Should Stop Setting Easy Goals. Harvard Business Review. [cited June 2019]. Available from: https://hbr.org/2018/11/why-you-should-stop-setting-easy-goals

(4) Pink, Daniel. (2018) When: The Scientific Secrets of Perfect Timing. Edinburgh: Cannongate Books.

(5) Kahneman, Daniel. (2012) Thinking, Fast and Slow. London: Penguin.

5.4 HOW TO APPLY

The first step is to identify our critical elements in relation to each win. Make a list of all the things that must be true in order to make that win possible.

Now we need to interrogate that list. Work through each critical element and ask two questions:

1. Do I need this in order to achieve my win?
2. Without this, will I be able to reach my win?

If this answer to question one is anything other than 'yes', then it is not a critical element and should be crossed off the list.

Likewise, if the answer to question two, is anything other than 'no', it is not a critical element and should be removed.

Bear in mind that some elements may seem essential when it comes to achieving the win, but will not actually make a big difference if they are not present. This exercise should be brutal – if only one or two critical elements are left on the list, that's OK.

Now we go a step further and work through the list asking ourselves "is this a fact or an opinion?". If it is an opinion, then we need to identify how we will obtain facts to decide if it is a true critical element or a "nice to have".

For instance, if our win is to complete The Three Peaks Challenge, our list of critical elements may look like this:

1. Need to be able to physically cover the distance
2. Need to have an all-weather kit
3. Need to have knowledge of the route
4. Need to be psychologically prepared for all conditions and terrain

Our marginal gains may include:

- Fitness
- Teamwork

- Access to a car/van
- Food
- Petrol money
- Overcoming tiredness
- Fear of failure
- Bad weather
- Proper clothing
- Raising money for charity

We can now split this list into 'knowns' and 'unknowns'. What do we know to be true? What do we need to research?

KNOWNS

- Fitness – essential to any exercise-based ambition.
- Access to a car/van – vital as a means of getting from one mountain to another.
- Petrol money – without this it won't be possible to refuel along the way.
- Bad weather – an 'unknown' entity – but we can plan for this by bringing waterproof and hi-vis clothing.
- Proper clothing – hiking boots are essential, along with weather-appropriate clothing that won't put us at risk of overheating or hypothermia.
- Food – climbing three mountains within 24 hours will only be possible with good nutrition.

UNKNOWNS

- Teamwork - it is technically possible to complete the challenge alone, but most people prefer to do it within a supportive and communicative team.
- Raising money for charity –The Three Peaks Challenge is often done in aid of charity. However, in this example, the completion of the challenge is the 'win', which suggests that raising money

for charity would be a happy bonus. If the stated win was to raise a certain amount of money for charity, this would be flipped, and The Three Peaks Challenge may become a critical element instead.

- Overcoming tiredness – this is very important, but ultimately not a dealbreaker. Tiredness is an expected outcome of staying awake for almost 24 hours and climbing three mountains in a row and it can be minimised in numerous ways.
- Fear of failure – this is an opinion, and can be overcome with confidence and a strong atomic foundation.

By interrogating our longlist, we have been left with six known marginal gains that are necessary in order for us to achieve our win of completing The Three Peaks Challenge.

Now, we take each element and break it down further.

So for instance, to fulfil the critical element of 'fitness' we may have to improve our exercise regime to ensure that we are capable of climbing three mountains in one day.

- What do we need to focus on? We should create a regime that will improve our leg strength.
- How do we achieve that? We can use the step machine at the gym.
- What are the risks? The step machine may be in use.
- How can we solve that problem? By adding the leg press into our regime, we have another exercise option while we wait for the step machine to become available.
- Now, using the leg press has become a new marginal gain – it is not crucial to the win, but it plays an important role in keeping us on track.

This process is used by professional athletes and C-suite executives across the world, and it works.

"As an athlete, it is common practice to set goals and our performance is often measured against whether or not we have achieved those goals," explains Hannah MacLeod. "For example, to score more goals in a season. Then I will sit down with a coach and review whether or not that's true or false.

"I know that by analysing and interrogating my performance goals, I will improve my performance and contribute to my confidence - my confidence being my belief in my ability to achieve."

Download the workbook for this chapter at: *WhatDoesItTakeToWin.com/workbook*

5.5 SUMMARY

Critical elements are essential in order for us to reach our win. But they can also be confusing. It is very easy to mistake a critical element for a marginal gain, or an opinion. This is why it is so important to interrogate each element and ensure that we are focusing only on the things that will help us to progress towards our win.

The benefits of ambitious goal-setting have been studied by athletes, businesses and academics over the course of many decades. It has been proven again and again that this works, but only if we are able to maintain our focus on the win. Each marginal gain and critical element can help us to stay focused. They arm us with a plan that will get us from where we are to where we want to be. They can also help us to identify the likely obstacles that lie in our way, so we can plan around them as well.

Of course, there will always be 'unknown' risks, but as long as we acknowledge these, we will be in a much stronger position to handle any unpredictable events that come our way.

By following this plan, we are giving ourselves the best possible chance of success, and the confidence that we need to reach that win in the end.

This is how our critical elements contribute to the clarity of the win. It may be hard work, but it may also be extremely rewarding.

Chapter 6

Planning
– What preparation is required to
increase the probability of success?

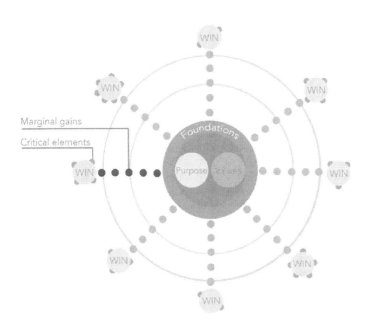

6.1 INTRODUCING PLANNING

Whether we are seeking wins in sport, business or life, preparation is everything. We have already conducted a pre-mortem on our win to help us identify any potential roadblocks on our way to success. We have also listed the critical elements that have to be in place before we can progress to our win, and the marginal gains which contribute to each element. In this chapter, we will learn how to future-proof our plans and handle any obstacles that might stand in our way.

We know what it's going to take to get to our win, now we just need to put in the work.

There are three components to this planning stage, where we learn what preparation is required to increase our probability of success.

These are:

- The timeline
- The test
- The marginal gains

The timeline helps us to stay on track and reminds us to keep visualising the moment of the win. It will be useful for us to use that moment as a vantage point from which we can take stock of our progress and the possible pitfalls that could create obstacles in our way.

The test forces us to face our fears so that they do not overwhelm us. We have to interrogate every possible problem that we may face, and then come up with a plan to solve them, long before they actually present themselves to us.

Finally, the marginal gains help us to stay focused without getting overwhelmed by the task at hand. We may find that there are one or two marginal gains which we choose to focus on, but each one represents an area of potential gain that deserves to be explored.

Once these three components are in place, the truly hard work begins. Good preparation involves imagining a series of worst-case scenarios and being brutally honest with ourselves about the role we play in them.

Let's say our win involves being in the starting line-up of a Premier League football club, what might stand in the way of that happening? If the worst-case scenario is being left on the subs bench, why might that become our reality? Is it something to do with our attitude? Our skill? Our fitness? This is an example of a controllable fear – if being benched is our worst-case scenario, we can minimise the risk of that happening by working harder and being a better team player. It is not going to come down to luck. However, there are a few uncontrollables that may lead us to be subbed. Maybe we were injured in the pre-season and haven't fully recovered in time for the first match of the League. This may not be something that we can necessarily control, but we can certainly try to minimise the risk of injury by warming up properly and avoiding dangerous situations off the pitch.

Preparation involves thinking about every single thing that could go right or wrong on the road to our win. Preparation gives us the confidence we need to succeed by forcing us to face our fears and take responsibility for our own shortcomings. This will involve hard work, but we have already come a long way through this process. We have a purpose, we know our values, we have set our foundations and we have clarity of our win. Now we just need to clear away the last remaining obstacles in our path so that we can reach our full potential.

6.2 DEFINING

When we plan, we are committing to see a project through. We are taking all of our learning to date, and applying it in realistic, practical terms to give ourselves the best possible chance of attaining our win.

Planning requires discipline. It also requires bravery. When we plan, we are telling ourselves what needs to happen and what needs to be avoided in order to make progress. Some of these things may fall outside of our comfort zone, and some actions may be downright scary, but we need to trust the process and take it step by step.

STEP ONE: The Timeline

Our timeline begins at the win date. This could be a graduation day, the start of a race, the ribbon-cutting ceremony at a new building, or the results announcement at local council elections.

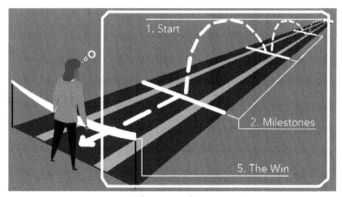

The timeline

For one particular Track Record client, the timeline was a self-set deadline of 12 months. He decided that he wanted to take a role on the leadership team, but he had a fear of public speaking and he knew that this fear was going to make him ineligible for the promotion.

He set public speaking as his priority and worked backwards in his timeline, marking out key milestones along the way. For instance, within three months he volunteered to deliver a small presentation at a company meeting. A month later he would speak at a school assembly and a month after that he would deliver a speech at a large industry conference.

Whatever we are working towards, when setting a timeline we have to start at the end of the track and work backwards.

We can already visualise the moment of our win, so now we need to take a step back. What happened the day before the win? What happened that week? If our win is to finish writing a book, we may need to spend several days proofreading for errors and checking for consistency. Now take another step back. One month before the book is finished, we may be writing the last couple of chapters. Three months before that we might be writing the first chapter. Six months before we finish the book, we might be creating the overall structure, the plot and the characters. We keep repeating this pattern one phase at a time until we are in the present day. Now we can identify the first step.

By starting at the end and working back, we make the win feel closer and more attainable. And by creating a timetable to this win, we can put together a plan that will guide us to the finish line.

STEP TWO: The test
Now we must once again interrogate our plans to ensure that they can withstand any risks, hurdles or blind spots along the way.

Overcoming obstacles in your path

This is the point at which we identify our major fears. What are we most afraid of? And how likely is it that it will happen? If our win was to write a book, we may be afraid that injury or illness could get in the way of our progress.

When he interrogated his fear of public speaking, the manager realised that his main concern was that he didn't come across well when speaking to large crowds. He was great one on one, but was too robotic when speaking in public. His priority was therefore to get better at his delivery and performance, and he planned to practice this by scheduling ever-larger public speaking engagements until he got it right.

We all need to be prepared to judge our behaviours in order to understand our fears. However, that doesn't mean that all fears are unfounded. We also need to think about the consequences for us if our fears became our reality. Injury or illness will certainly affect the timeline of the win, and it may force us to change the way we work. A broken hand will mean it is impossible to type. So, what can we do to mitigate this risk? If we do in fact break our hand, we could always record our voice dictating the content on our phone, and find an app or service to transcribe it.

We should always take the time to figure out the root cause of our fears. Why are we afraid of injury? Is this something that has happened before? Are we particularly at risk of a certain illness?

We can also use this test to minimise these risks and hurdles where possible. For example, we can look after our wellness by avoiding situations where we are likely to be injured, and by leading a healthy lifestyle to improve our immune system. We can then protect ourselves even further by preparing back-up plans which we can fall back on should our worst fears become our reality.

STEP THREE: Marginal gains
We already know the value of tracking our marginal gains - these are the components of each critical element that will deliver improvements if addressed daily, weekly or monthly until they bring us all the way to our end win.

Each marginal gain should correspond with one of our critical elements, they should be listed in order of priority so that we can use our time as efficiently as possible.

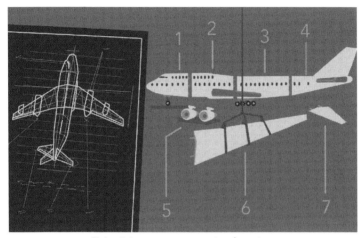

Prioritise your marginal gains

In the last chapter, we analysed the value of our marginal gains so this step should simply confirm them and ensure that we are treating them with the correct level of priority. Again, to take the book example, one marginal gain may be to invest in a good computer, while another may be to schedule regular breaks to keep our mind fresh. Which of these marginal gains is going to be more helpful in getting us to our win? And how do we make sure we achieve that gain?

The business manager with the fear of public speaking addressed his fears in public until he became more confident. He was very clear about the things that he had to develop through marginal gains and he prioritised them in terms of urgency. He had the clarity of what he needed to achieve to get to his win and he created his own opportunities to develop them. He sought feedback and took it where possible. He ended up achieving his win ahead of schedule – he joined the leadership team within nine months, rather than twelve.

We can never guarantee our success, but we can always increase the chances of it happening. Performance excellence begins when we make a choice to succeed at something which is completely within our control. We commit to that choice, and then we visualise the win.

Committing to the win

Commitment is not merely a state of mind – it is evident in our actions. We can only say we are "committed" when we demonstrate repeatedly our determination to carry out our actions to the best of our ability and demonstrate an unwillingness to give up in the face of obstacles. Committed people are typically tied both intellectually and emotionally to their values and goals; they know they have the competence to perform the jobs that are expected of them.

When we have established the direction we want to take, committing to that decision requires persistence and change. Planning helps to remove the factors in our environment that may hold us back, and it can also help us to overcome the fears that can sometimes paralyse us. It can also act as a mechanism to help hold us accountable when times are tough and obstacles get in the way.

Most people fail to commit because they want certainty. They want to know that making a commitment to change will definitely result in the outcome they are striving to achieve. The reality is that often there is little certainty in a complex world. However, embracing the uncertainty that comes with pursuing your end win and being comfortable with change are important skills. Again, we can think about the 'known unknowns' and 'unknown unknowns'. There are certain eventualities that we can predict and attempt to minimise – like the probability of David's pre-Olympics injury, but there will always be a few unexpected obstacles along the way that we have to adapt to. While we can't predict every hurdle, we can give ourselves the best possible chance of surviving them by understanding our core values and foundations, and creating a template for success that we can return to at any point.

Overcoming fear of failure

When we can accept the potential challenges or fears that could limit our future success, we can use our fear of failure to our advantage.

"Jane is a female executive at a FTSE 100 firm who came to Track Record with a fear-based work situation," says Track Record's Katherine Moore.

"She was told she was getting a new boss in a role that implied a slight demotion, and she was asked to interview the woman who was set to take this role. In her mind, that first meeting went really badly. Her perception was that it wasn't her interviewing the potential candidate, it was the other way around – she felt that her potential new boss was questioning her work ethic and picking holes in her processes.

"In their second meeting, Jane got the impression that her potential boss didn't trust her, and didn't think that she was particularly good at her job.

"When we exported where that feeling was coming from we found that Jane's fear was that she was going to lose her job because she would be seen as being inadequate. She was worried that this new boss would micro manage her.

"When we explored where that was coming from, we asked her when she might have felt like this before. She realised that she had had a female boss previously and she did all of those things to her – she micro managed her, she didn't trust her, and she made her feel like she wasn't good at her job.

"As a result, Jane had embedded the belief that she did not trust female bosses. This was all being projected onto this new woman. When she said it out loud, she realised it was a totally irrational idea. It was a limiting belief borne from fear.

"We were able to reframe Jane's fear as an opportunity to gain from this woman's experience and learn from her. In this way it could be a positive experience.

"Jane went into the next meeting and it was a positive interaction. Six months later, she was still with the company and much happier in her role."

Fear is a basic human emotion. It is hard-wired into our systems for a beneficial purpose - to alert us to danger and prepare us physically to accomplish what is necessary for survival. But while fear is a vital resource in times of danger, in the modern world, it can have significant negative influences on the choices we make.

Fear typically results in a common pattern of behaviour. Fear only allows us to see the negatives in a given situation and identifies the worst that could happen. It drives impulsive behaviour and makes it difficult to step back and assess a situation. Fear tells us to avoid anything new or unknown. It prefers that we stay in our comfort zone.

Whether it is the fear of public speaking, fear of pursuing a life-long ambition, of failure or of what others may think of us, it is not the actual fear that is holding us back – it is the anticipation of that fear. Fear causes us to conjure up a series of worst-case scenarios that appear to have no positive interpretation. Ahead of a public speaking engagement, it is easy to think: "I can't do this, I'm going to forget my words and everyone will laugh at me." Yet in reality, this is unlikely to happen, we have all witnessed speeches that have not been perfectly delivered, and most of the time those mistakes go unnoticed by everyone except the speaker. In the rare cases where the audience spots the error, they are probably going to go with the flow, rather than laugh us off the stage. And if they do laugh, we can turn this to our advantage by coming prepared with a joke to ease the tension and win back the room. Or alternatively, we can avoid this whole scenario completely by planning out our speech in advance and bringing notes with us.

Fear can make us stronger, more capable people, just as long as we treat it as an opportunity instead of a hurdle.

On the eve of the 2008 Australian Open Tennis final, tennis legend Billie Jean King sent a text message to Maria Sharapova, "Champions take chances. Pressure is a privilege." (1) This simple message helped put the task of winning into perspective. Sharapova accepted the inevitable anxiety caused by appearing in the final of the Australian Open and found the courage and trust in herself to cope with the occasion.

The phrase "pressure is a privilege" helped shift focus from what might have been an uncomfortable or stressful experience, to something much more positive. This reframing of focus – to choose to focus on the ultimate win and what will go right, instead of worrying about what can go wrong or what's out of our control, is critical when it comes to achieving performance excellence.

Sharapova went on to win the 2008 Australian Open Final.

When David Carry was injured just a few weeks before the Olympic trials, he was able to minimise the disruption to his training schedule thanks to proper planning. His coaching team had already identified that David could be vulnerable to a particular type of back injury, due to his age, his body shape, the event he was competing in, and the fact that his training was very focused on improving his under-water kick. The results of this pre-mortem found that a lower back injury posed a risk to David during training. The team was then able to put some measures in place to reduce the risk of this injury, and they also put together a plan to deal with this injury if it did end up happening.

A few weeks before the Olympic trials, David suffered from a bulging disk in his lower back, but because he had already put a recovery plan in place, it did not end his Olympic dreams.

"That change in approach meant that I actually improved on my best ever performance by a significant margin," says David. "My biggest fear had come true and yet it improved my performance because we were confident in our approach."

According to the Nobel Prize Laureate Daniel Kahneman (2), conducting a thorough pre-mortem rewards people for finding flaws in their existing plans. The result of this approach is an increase in the collective confidence to perform, especially when in reality we are faced with previously identified and considered challenges.

However, this is easier said than done. By confronting our fears and identifying previously unknown hurdles, we will be forced to make at least a few changes to our plans, and this can feel destabilising.

We need to build the expectation of change into our plans so that we don't allow it to get in the way of our win. Expecting resistance to change and planning for it from the start is a proactive step.

Three questions which help to recognise behaviours that indicate possible resistance are:

- What are we avoiding?
- What are the fears holding us back?
- What beliefs do we hold that might not be true?

Part of our commitment to planning should include exploring the language we use, the fears we hold on to, the stories we tell ourselves and the behaviours we display every day. These are within our control and provide a vital source of confidence. It is vital that we rely on this source of confidence, rather than pinning our hopes on extrinsic factors to offer validation. The roar of the crowd or the rush of closing a big sale should be viewed as positive add-ons, rather than forming the bedrock of our confidence. We are unlikely to be able to control other people's behaviours or their responses to our actions, but if we focus our energy on the areas we can control - such as our thoughts and actions – we can increase the chance of success.

6.3 SCIENCE AND EVIDENCE

Preparing for success involves a lot of complex, worst-case scenario planning. We do this at the start of our journey so that we aren't caught off guard at a crucial point on our path to the win. Psychologist Gary Klein's (3) pre-mortem theory is a great illustration of how valuable it can be to imagine the worst in order to prevent it from happening, and Daniel Kahneman used this theory as a springboard for his award-winning book Thinking Fast and Slow (2). But Kahneman and Klein are not the only scholars to have studied these patterns of human thought, and how they can be manipulated to bring success.

Academics Gardner and Moore (4) wrote that "committed action" can result in success, but only if that commitment comes from the right place. In chapter two, we looked at the importance of values, and it is this value-driven behaviour that will help us to make the right commitments in the planning stage.

Committed action is easiest when we are doing something that aligns with our own values. Placing our values to the forefront of our mind provides motivation when there is no external reward, energy is low or frustrations are high. Whether we are seeking a promotion at work, starting out a new exercise regime or embarking on a new phase in our personal lives, there will always be a point where things just feel frustrating and hard. Our values act as our filter in these moments, guiding us towards the win. By acting in a way that is true to our values, we can overcome the negative thoughts and external challenges that threaten to derail our journey to the win. These negative elements will inevitably emerge at some point along the way, and they can mean the difference between obtaining the win and giving up. Accounting for these setbacks in the planning stage can help us prepare, and this preparation can even be an empowering tool that helps us to confront our fear of failure.

Controlling the controllables

As philosopher Gregory Bateson said, "Nothing exists without context." (5) But unfortunately, a lot of decisions are made without first understanding the underlying context and environment. Understanding different contexts goes a long way towards making sense of situations and improving our decision-making capabilities.

Reality is subjective and each person has their own unique perception of the world, no two people have the exact same understanding of what is real. Therefore, theoretical models can be useful to provide a metaphor to structure, organise, understand and interpret perceived reality. In his book 'The Edge of Organisation' (6), Russ Marion argues that we function best when we can find that sweet spot between the complexity of chaos and the discipline of organisation. He uses this theory to explain evolution, stating:

"Full-blown Chaotic Systems flit a bit too readily from novelty to novelty; living systems need to consolidate gains. Predictable, stable systems, by contrast, possess none of the panache needed to create new order or even to respond adaptively to creative environments. Complex Systems lie between these poles, at the Edge of Chaos, and they have both panache and stability sufficient to serve life." (6)

According to Marion, a little bit of chaos is necessary for our growth, but only if it is tempered by more structured and academic viewpoints. In other words, we function best when we accept that we have no control over the uncontrollables, while also controlling the controllables as well as we can. If we can do that, we can turn those 'unknowns' or 'uncontrollables' into learning experiences. Accepting our occasional unpreparedness is a big part of this preparation stage.

The academics David Snowden and Mary Boone

created The Cynefin Framework (7) to explain the complexity between the predictable world and the unpredictable world. The diagram, seen in Figure 6.1, was once described by Snowden as a "sense-making device". It shows the four different domains that help to explain our own and other people's behaviours and motivations.

These domains are: complex, knowable, chaotic, and known

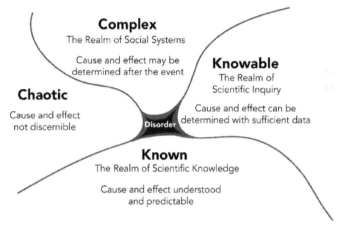

Complex
The Realm of Social Systems

Cause and effect may be
determined after the event

Knowable
The Realm of
Scientific Inquiry

Chaotic

Cause and effect
not discernible

Disorder

Cause and effect can be
determined with sufficient data

Known
The Realm of Scientific Knowledge

Cause and effect understood
and predictable

Figure 6.1 Reprinted by permission of Harvard Business Review.
Exhibit from "A Leader's Framework for Decision Making" by Snowden and Boone November 2007.
Copyright ©2019 by Harvard Business Publishing; all rights reserved. (7)

The domains offer a 'sense of place' from which to analyse behaviour and make decisions within a variety of situations. In the 'known' domain, the relationships between cause and effect are well understood. They are repeatable, and because we have repeated experience of them, we have learned the underlying relationships and behaviours sufficiently well that the consequences of any course of action can be predicted with near certainty. In such contexts, decision making tends to take the form of recognising patterns and responding to them with well-rehearsed actions. For example, an army officer leading routine training through a forest will know exactly what is expected of them at any given point, because they have researched and planned every step of the exercise.

In the knowable domain, cause and effect relationships are generally understood, but for any specific decision there is a need to gather and analyse further data before the consequences of any course of action can be predicted with any certainty. This is the domain in which to apply the standard methods of operational research and decision analysis. So, the army officer who is leading the training exercise may wish to account for the inclusion of some new recruits, who may have a disruptive effect on the other soldiers, slowing down the whole team as a result. This is a knowable problem which can be accounted for in advance.

In the complex domain, decision-making situations involve many interacting causes and effects. Knowledge is at best qualitative: there are simply too many potential interactions to disentangle particular causes and effects. Every situation has unique elements: some novel or unfamiliar.

Decision support will be more focused on exploring judgement and issues, and on developing broad strategies that are flexible enough to accommodate changes as the situation evolves. To illustrate, during the army officer's training exercise, the team encounters a forest fire. This requires a change in schedule as they call the emergency services, attempt to contain the fire and alert civilians to the risks, and then navigate a new route through the forest.

In the chaotic domain, situations involve events and behaviours beyond our current experience and there are no obvious candidates for cause and effect. Decision making cannot be based upon analysis because there are no concepts of how to separate entities and predict their interactions. Decision makers will need to take probing actions and see what happens, until they can make some sort of sense of the situation, gradually drawing the context back into one of the other domains. Let's say the discovery that the forest fire was started intentionally, and the direction of the flames is threatening the natural habitat of an endangered animal. This development creates chaos by introducing an unknown entity operating with an unclear intent, and unpredictable results. It is an 'unknown unknown' which forces us to act impulsively and perhaps even in opposition to our prepared actions.

In reality, there is a lot of natural movement between the different domains of the Cynefin Framework. This movement usually goes in a clockwise direction through the emergence of stabilisation and ordering of ideas, through the definition, hypothesis formulation and testing of solutions to knowable problems, until known solutions are implemented as part of the everyday ritual.

By following the Cynefin Framework we can mimic the predictabilities and the unpredictabilities of life, by applying different situations to the framework in order to test our reactions to each one. Testing our assumptions and pursuing reality in a complex environment requires the skill of listening to learn. This challenges us to build flexibility into our plans to account for those unexpected delays or distractions.

In preparation for the Rio Olympic Games, the Women's Great Britain Hockey Team looked at every aspect of performance, the environmental challenges and strategies within their control that could help mitigate any potential drags. The team knew that they were facing a potential 90-minute commute to get from the athlete's village to the match venue. With a game played every other day, players were becoming concerned with the negative impact this would have on their recovery.

However, with the guidance of the coaches and

psychologist, the team chose to focus on what was within their control. They looked at using portable fridges to store their recovery food on the bus, battery operated recovery pumps for the players to wear whilst seated on the bus – all the way down to the detail of whether music should be played or if it was best to have peace and quiet!

This planning and discussion reduced anxiety and the fear of the unknown, thereby giving a sense of control and confidence. Discussing a variety of possible outcomes, however remote they seemed, gave the team the advantage of being prepared in advance for almost any situation they could encounter.

REFERENCES

(1) Matthews, B. 'Billie Jean King text helps inspire new queen'. Herald Sun (digital). 2008, January 26. Available at: https://www.heraldsun.com.au/sport/tennis/kings-words-inspire-sharapova/news-story/a44208d3bee37b96010deb4960810e18 [viewed June 2019]

(2) Kahneman D. (2013). Thinking Fast and Slow. New York: Penguin Group

(3) Klein, G. (2008). Performing a Project Premortem. IEEE Engineering Management Review. June 2008 Issue. Available at: https://www.researchgate.net/publication/3229642_Performing_a_Project_Premortem [viewed June 2019].

(4) Gardner, F. L. & Moore, Z. E. (2007). The Psychology of Enhancing Human Performance: The Mindfulness-Acceptance-Commitment (MAC) Approach. New York: Springer Publishing Company. P.291-299.

(5) Bateson, Gregory (2003). 'New Science' in the Context of Communicology. The American Journal of Semiotics, Issue 1. Available at: https://www.academia.edu/10361896/Gregory_Batesons_New_Science_in_the_Context_of_Communicology. [Viewed June 2019].

(6) Marion, R. (1999). The Edge of Organization: Chaos and Complexity Theories of Formal Social Systems. Thousand Oaks, CA: Sage Publications. P.xiv

(7) Snowden and Boone (2007). A Leader's Framework for Decision Making. Harvard Business Review, November 2007 Issue. Available at: https://hbr.org/2007/11/a-leaders-framework-for-decision-making [viewed June 2019].

6.4 HOW TO APPLY

"In preparing for battle, I have always found that plans are useless, but planning is indispensable." – General Dwight D. Eisenhower

Our confidence is easily knocked when we aren't properly prepared. And this includes the ability to prepare for the unexpected – to build a cushion into our plans to account for those chaotic and complex scenarios.

We must try to identify any risks, barriers or hurdles that might stand between us and our win, and then we need to analyse the possible causes and consequences of those fears coming true. By doing this we can work to reduce these risks or at least minimise the consequences if the worst case scenario does happen.

At Track Record, we work with individuals and teams to help them make the most of this planning stage.

We start by asking a series of questions:

*   What is your purpose, identity and end win? By reminding ourselves of this, we are able to stay focused and committed even during times of instability.

Exercise: Reinforcing commitment

Purpose	Identity	End Win

*   What external future factors might affect our world? This could be anything from injury, to geo-political risks, to extreme weather conditions, to personal issues.

Exercise: External factors

Impacting factors

• What people, businesses and institutions will we be interacting with on our journey? By identifying these outlying factors, we may be able to identify other new risks and possible solutions ahead of time.

Exercise: Outlying factors

Outlying Factors

• What are our major fears?

Exercise: Identifying fears

My fears

Now that we have this information, we can make a long list of our fears and risk factors, and identify each one as being either controllable or uncontrollable.

Exercise: Controllable or uncontrollable?

Fear	Controllable or uncontrollable?	Risk Factor	Controllable or uncontrollable?

We have to take a 'future-back' approach to tackle these fears. We imagine ourselves at the point of the win, and we look around us.

So, if that win was to move to another country for an exciting new job, we would begin by visualising our ideal life abroad – where are we living? Who are we with? What do we do for fun? How do we feel?

Let's assume there is a different way of looking at this. What else might happen in this future? If we don't thrive in the job, what then? Are we still living abroad? Do we stay in the job and get our fulfilment elsewhere? Do we feel differently as a result?

Try to imagine at least three possible scenarios where we have attained our win, but in a slightly different way to what we had imagined. In each new iteration of this dream, try to change one key controllable factor and one uncontrollable factor and see how the situation plays out. Suppose that, we take the job, move abroad, then use it as a stepping stone to an even better job back in our home country again. Alternatively, we take the job, move abroad, and then a close family member becomes ill back home and needs our help.

Exercise: Different outcomes

	Win version 1	Win version 2	Win version 3
Controllable			
Uncontrollable			

The more possibilities we consider, the more we can prepare, and that preparation period gives us the confidence that we are going to need to progress towards the win.

- When we are thinking about these various options, we should ask:
- What assumptions are we making that may be limiting our options?
- What would be the emotional cost of making this choice?
- If all of these options end in failure, what else could we do?

In the exercise 'minimalising risk', we will break down each of our critical elements into a series of potential challenges. These challenges can be either known or unknown and are designed to make us troubleshoot our fears.

List each critical element along with at least four potential challenges, and then think about how that challenge could be handled. Finally, write down your choice – the way you have chosen to handle this particular fear.

To give you an idea, if your win was to buy your first home, one critical element would be to save for a deposit. A potential challenge may be an unexpected cost, such as new car, which would force you to dip into your house savings.

This risk could be minimised by ensuring that your car is regularly serviced and always driven carefully. You could make the choice to drive less to minimise the risk of any damage while you are saving for your house deposit. Or you may decide that it would be cheaper in the long term to sell your car and invest in a newer model that will require less maintenance. Think about the choice that you are prepared to make, and write it in the box as a commitment to yourself.

Exercise: Minimalising risk

CRITICAL ELEMENT 1	Potential challenge	How can we minimise/ mitigate this risk?	CHOICE
CRITICAL ELEMENT 2	Potential challenge	How can we minimise/ mitigate this risk?	CHOICE
CRITICAL ELEMENT 3	Potential challenge	How can we minimise/ mitigate this risk?	CHOICE

To prevent a fear from sabotaging our opportunity to learn and develop, research has shown that visualising fears or future obstacles results in individuals feeling more energised, confident and able to accomplish more than individuals who rely on making decisions based on delusional optimism.

Proactively identifying potential fears, negative outcomes and events, with the purpose of creating a more robust and measured approach, is essential.

Download the workbook for this chapter at: *WhatDoesItTakeToWin.com/workbook*

6.5 SUMMARY

By planning properly for our win, we are giving ourselves the best possible chance of actually getting there. But proper preparation is not easy. There are no short cuts here, and we have to be meticulous in our approach to identifying obstacles and risks.

Perhaps the hardest thing of all is facing our fears. For most of us, fear of failure is what holds us back from pursuing our wins. This same fear drains us of our confidence, making it less likely that we will progress to that end win.

Fear can be a great motivator, but it can also hold us back. We need to use this planning stage to come to terms with our own overriding fears and then do everything in our power to prevent them from taking over. As Billie Jean King said, pressure is a privilege. We are only afraid of the failure because the win means so much. We can use this fact to push ourselves a little bit harder to identify the reasons for our fears and cancel them out by including failure in our plans.

We already have all the tools at our disposal to do this; it's just a matter of discipline. By taking control of our negative thoughts and feelings, we can reduce their impact on our win and save our energy for our critical elements, the actions that will actually help propel us forward, rather than dragging us to a standstill.

When our priorities are in order and our plan is in place, there will be no stopping us.

Chapter 7

Execution
- Identify the link between mindset,
attitude and behaviour so being our
best more often becomes a choice.

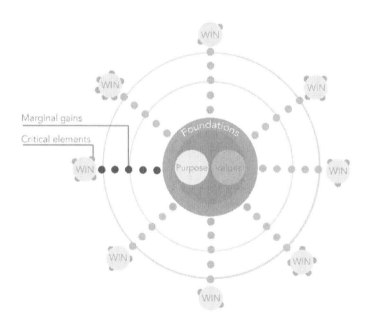

7.1 INTRODUCING THE EXECUTION...

This is how our thoughts become our reality

It's July 2012. David Carry is standing at the edge of an Olympic-sized pool, in front of an Olympic-sized crowd. He has just recovered from a painful back injury, but will go on to compete in the 400m freestyle finals, finishing in seventh place.

That was David's moment of execution. He had established his goal, decided to achieve it, and planned for every possible eventuality that might stand in his way. This meant that at the moment of execution, he simply had to believe in himself and get into the right mindset for the competition ahead. But this is a lot harder than it might seem.

This is a hallmark of any great athlete. Think of Roger Federer during a game of tennis, or Cristiano Ronaldo on a football pitch. Their seemingly effortless achievements are the result of their ability to become unconsciously highly responsive during the game following intensive mental and physical training. This means they can deliver the best possible outcome by ensuring that their response to the demands of the situation is their very best.

Like David, Roger and Cristiano, we can deliver the outcomes we wish to achieve in our lives by shaping our response to our environment. So, in this chapter we will learn what it takes to achieve our win by putting into practice everything that we have already learned.

How does mindset and belief impact our attitude and behaviour? And how can we use mindset and belief to bring us to the point of execution, and beyond?

Your behaviours are learnt from birth and they are constantly being reinforced through habits.

Many are there for self protection, both physically (tiger = run) and emotionally (personal criticism = self justification).

Most of us are caught in a habit loop that is doing us no favours. We hear a sudden noise and we jump, despite knowing that we are not in a dangerous situation. We receive constructive criticism and we take it personally, attacking ourselves for not getting it perfect the first time around. These reactions may seem natural, but that doesn't mean that we are powerless to control them. We simply need to experience the moment of realisation which allows us to break the habit loop and change our internal narrative.

The habit loop has four elements that form a feedback loop, running constantly throughout our lives, as shown in figure 7.1

The Habit Loop

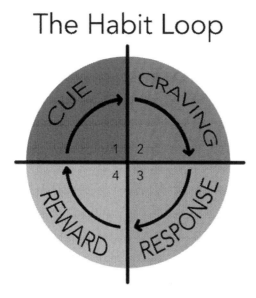

Figure 7.1. The Habit Loop (1)

It starts with a cue that automatically triggers our brain to use a habit, the response. The response could be physical, such as jumping at a loud noise. Or it could be emotional – feeling upset by a co-worker's comment. The reward tells your brain that the habit should be remembered. Once the habit is formed, we get a craving to make the response after the cue because our brain knows that we will receive the reward.

Every decision is born out of a realisation that something must change. And applying that decision requires a commitment to breaking the habit loop for less positive habits and positive habit formation. In doing this, we can prepare ourselves to take on the day to day challenges that move us closer to our goals. It's about making better choices more often and the ability to learn and review to increase our chances of achieving powerful wins in life, business and sport.

Before he was able to change his mindset and performance, David had to accept a few hard truths. "I was a top ten ranked athlete, but I was unaware of quite how bad my turns were," he says. "My turn time was not even in the top 100 in the world! It was my belief that turns were not critical to my overall outcome, that it was fitness and swimming technique that would be the most important aspects of my race. It meant that when it came to practicing turns during training, I just went through the motions and so when I competed at the Olympics, the outcome of my turns was the outcome I deserved.

"The realisation moment came when I was presented with data and video evidence where I realised how bad I was against my competitors. For 75% of my race, the swimming part, I was the second quickest in the world, after Michael Phelps. But for the other 25% of the race, the turns and dive, I was terrible!

"After I got over that ego hit, I was able to see that I just needed to become average at my turns to have a positive impact on my performance. It took a great deal of understanding the biomechanics, physical and psychological aspects of where I could improve, and then it took a great deal of effort and intensity to make these improvements.

"It was incredibly difficult to re-learn something that had been so natural to me, albeit ineffectual. Ultimately, I was able to dramatically improve my turn technique and so my overall swimming performance."

This was how David created a positive habit, by understanding what response, improved turns, led to a reward, improved times.

As we shall see, achieving substantial wins requires an intense information-gathering process. It's not easy, but it is a proven way to get to your own version of the London 2012 Olympics, whether that's a promotion at work, a new personal best (PB) on the track, or financial security. If you are eyeing up a truly aspirational win, you can be certain it's not going to be plain sailing between where we are now and where we want to be. We are going to have to discover and consider ideas we didn't even know existed. We will have to test ideas, expose hidden weaknesses, and understand the subconscious subroutines that are standing in our way. And we need to experience failures so we can learn from them again and again.

The journey to implementation starts by clarifying the beliefs we hold and how they affect mindset and attitude. When we are truly honest about these things, we can adjust our behaviour accordingly to navigate the challenges that we face. In this chapter, we will map out this whole approach, then apply it systematically by integrating it into our daily life through positive habit formation. Without the structure and discipline of this approach it can often be too easy to let go of the dream, to consider it too hard and to quit in order to protect ourselves from the fear of failure.

David did not arrive at the Olympics because of chance. His journey to London 2012 began in July 2005, when London was named as the 2012 host. He knew that he wanted to represent his country in his homeland. He knew that this would require long hours of training and extraordinary sacrifice. But it was not until he got to grips with his mindset and beliefs that he started to realise his full potential, as he continues his story:

"The biggest overall lesson for me was when I got to the 2012 London Olympics. I had achieved a personal best time and broken the over-30s world record by two and a half seconds and I was about to swim in the Olympic final of the 400 meters freestyle. It was my first ever Olympic final and no 30-year-old had ever made an Olympic final in that event before. It was also a home Olympics in front of 17,000 people and my family was in the stand. The video of me walking out was pretty amazing. I remember not just hearing the sound but feeling the sound as I walked out. I was actually the first British athlete at the Olympic Games to walk out on poolside in the Olympic final, so I was walking into the unknown. And wow did I feel it! It was the perfect ending to my career."

In this chapter we examine the science of how our mindset and beliefs determine our attitude and behaviour so we can experience with greater focus our perception of the world and the challenges before us. Understanding the science can help us influence our sympathetic and parasympathetic nervous system to allow us to hack into our own systems and make the changes that we need to make in order to deliver our best performance.

From our experience of coaching people through this process, it all comes down to mindset and belief, attitude, and behaviour.

In order to achieve something you have not yet done, you will need to change, adapt and evolve. This takes:

1. Realisation to identify what change is required.
2. Habit formation to make the change stick. Neither are easy, otherwise you would have done it already.

Both take focus and energy.

7.2 DEFINING

In the introduction we learned that changing habits and making improvements to become your best is a choice and that we can exponentially increase our ability to achieve this through self-awareness and the willingness to change. Events are often out of our control, but we can always control our response. That response, in turn, influences the outcome of the situation. We all have the capacity to shape our own outcomes by taking charge of our response – it is just a matter of understanding the process.

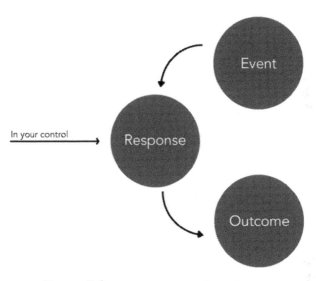

Figure 7.2 response, event, outcome

But how can we ensure that our response is designed to create the best possible outcome? It all comes down to three key elements: mindset, attitude and behaviour. The diagram in Figure 7.3 shows how mindset, attitude and behaviour are connected. Our mindset sets the tone and tells us what sort of attitude we should adopt to a particular situation. This attitude is actioned through our behaviour, and our behaviour – or response – influences the outcome, and may even lead to the creation of a brand new event.

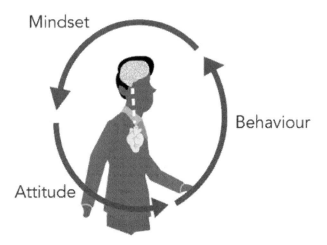

Figure 7.3 Mindset, attitude and behaviour

1. Behaviour

Of the three elements, behaviour is the simplest and the easiest for us to control. It is the way in which we conduct ourselves, particularly in relation to others. The external perception of our identity is strongly driven by our behaviour - if our behaviour is inconsistent, people will perceive our identity and beliefs as inconsistent. This can have a significant effect on the impact you can create.

Figure 7.4 shows The Betaris Concept, which highlights how attitude and behaviour are linked.

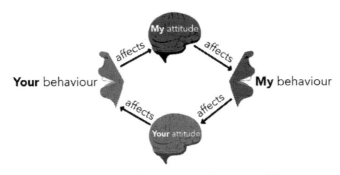

Figure 7.4 The Betaris Concept (2)

The Betaris Concept shows how our feelings and emotions influence our actions and reactions, which other people then observe, creating their perception of us. It demonstrates how important attitude is in creating an impression on other people, and influencing our own behaviour.

The fact that people are not their behaviour is not necessarily something that others will be aware of. The perceptions they form will influence their feelings and emotions, which influences their behaviour in response, and round and round it goes. For instance, a colleague may appear to be anxious and fearful in large meetings, leading them to avoid these situations and sit quietly without contributing. But when asked to confront this behaviour, the colleague realises that it was a result of being told to be quiet throughout childhood. What other members of the organisation could have interpreted as antisocial behaviour, was actually a defence mechanism that can be easily addressed.

We should remember that our interpretation of other people's behaviour contributes to our perception of them and their beliefs. But just as our behaviour does not necessarily represent us, the behaviour of others may not present an accurate portrayal of their true beliefs. It is important to note that if we can take control of our own behaviour, we are significantly more likely to represent our true identity and who we want to be in an authentic way that we can feel proud of and that is representative of the performance we want to give.

The components that drive behaviour are the keys to understanding and modifying behaviour. We may say to ourselves that we don't like a particular behaviour and commit to making a change. However, unless we pull back the curtain to reveal the core belief that underlies the behaviour, and how it could be limiting us, it can be near-impossible to make the adjustment in our behaviour.

Changing our behaviour requires us to mentally strip things right back to ask: "Why do I even believe this in the first place?" Is our behaviour driven by a desire to impress, or a fear of failure? Or have we never really given our behaviour much thought to begin with?

Most people never give themselves the time or space to consider why they behave the way they do. But the upside is that once we have identified the limiting belief, we can absolutely control the image that we present to others externally, while changing then reinforcing our own beliefs internally. This opens up a world of choice that we can direct and control.

2.   Attitude

According to the Oxford English Dictionary, attitude is simply a "settled way of thinking or feeling about something". Once we understand this, we can start to change our attitude through repetition and reinforcement of new thoughts and feelings, as shown in figure 7.5.

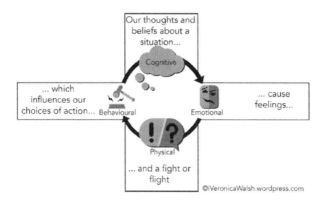

Figure 7.5 The cycle of attitude, thoughts and beliefs (3)

One of Mahatma Gandhi's most famous quotes asserted that our thoughts are the primary driver of our resulting behaviour.

"Your beliefs become your thoughts,
Your thoughts become your words,
Your words become your actions,
Your actions become your habits,
Your habits become your values,
Your values become your destiny."
-Mahatma Gandhi

This is why it is so important to spend a great deal of time focused on developing mindset and belief – it truly is at the root of every action and behaviour.

Having said that, us humans are very good at mistaking our feelings for a fact or reality that we are experiencing in that moment. For instance, we might conclude that because we feel scared about a task, that therefore that task is scary. Or we might think: "I feel I am not good enough" and therefore "I am not good enough and I cannot do the task at hand". In the world of sports, there are plenty of opportunities to bow out of a challenge because we don't think we can accomplish it – few people find themselves mid-way through a marathon thinking that it's easy. Our attitude can have a significant impact on performance until we learn the truth about how our feelings actually form.

Emotions are instinctive and powerful, so it is easy to mistake them for factual representations of our surroundings. For instance, while standing on that diving platform at the London 2012 Olympics, it is perfectly reasonable that David may have felt worry, fear, pressure, and pride. But in the stripped back reality of the world around him, he was merely a man standing by a pool, preparing to swim. If he had allowed himself to become consumed by worry, for instance, he may never have made it off the diving block – and if he had, his performance would have undoubtedly suffered as a result of the anxious thoughts flooding his mind.

There have been many scientific and academic studies completed on the impact that feelings can have on our real-life experience. We have all experienced this in our own lives – through a miscommunication that led to an unnecessary dispute, or a missed opportunity that we tell ourselves was our own fault.

The reality is our feelings are created and shaped by our thoughts. Our feelings are shaped purely by our perception of an experience. Once we know this, we can go through a step by step process to alter our attitude.

Ask yourself, is this thought a fact or a feeling? If you do not feel that you are good enough, what sort of training do you need to change that reality?

Gandhi said that positive thoughts can lead to a positive destiny, and his words continue to ring true. We are not the sum total of our thoughts or feelings. If we insist on entertaining only positive thoughts, this will lead to a positive feeling and that feeling will allow us to focus on the excitement of our goal and the joy of achieving it. In this way, a change in attitude can have a huge effect on our behaviour and – yes – our destiny.

3.   Mindset

The third element is your mindset, a combination of the beliefs that tell us who we are, what we're capable of and many other things. The danger with our beliefs is they feel like reality and that feeling is hard to shake. That is, until we realise that some of our beliefs are wrong.

The psychotherapist Amy Morin says that "if you draw inaccurate conclusions about who you are and what you're capable of doing, you'll limit your potential." In other words, the better we know ourselves, the better the chance we have of reaching our win.

It is essential to develop a deep understanding of our identity and a self-awareness of our mindset. It is also important to recognise that our beliefs are not who we are. This is especially true with negative beliefs, many of which are originally hard-wired into us as children by others who had no real understanding of what our abilities would become. Some of our strongest beliefs can be negative and self-deprecating and have very limiting effects on our capacity to perform. We may have been repeatedly told that we cannot achieve something and eventually we came to believe it.

The fixed idea that 'we are what we are and that's it' is scientifically wrong and has no place in a professional discussion around performance. It is through accepting the flexibility to change our beliefs that we can truly grow and change. The objective is to disconnect from our old belief systems and upgrade our negative, self-limiting beliefs by developing a flexible mindset which is constantly asking the right questions and challenging assumptions in the right way. Then we can identify which of our beliefs are totally based on fact versus opinion, against our perception of an event that we've retold until we start to believe it. This is a process that requires conscious effort and dedication, with time set aside for reflection.

David's final words on taking control show how our courageous decisions, even unlikely ones where not doing something leads to the right outcomes, are underpinned by the right attitude with a mindset that is composed of the right beliefs:

"I had to beat everybody else in the world to be able to get into the final and then I had to go again just a matter of hours later. I went into that final absolutely exhausted. I remember diving in and thinking "Wow, this is going to hurt", and it did. I just did not have anything left in the tank. The following day I spent all day in bed doing anything I could to recover. Two days later I had the relay heats in the 200 metres freestyle. I was second going into that relay and I remember diving in and thinking "Oh my God": I felt like a rusty Tin Man. My body was absolutely crushed from competing in the final three days earlier.

"The relay went okay. We got into the final. We were in good shape, but I just remember touching the wall and knowing that I didn't have anything left. I knew that that was everything I could give, and to get up and go again that night, I just had nothing left. Nothing at all. I remember going to the warm-up pool and up to the head coach and saying 'I know this is going to be my last ever race, but I've got nothing left: I really think I should step down and not swim in the final. You have the reserves. One of them should go in my place.

"I had missed medals in the 2004 and 2008 Olympics. Now here I was at London 2012. It was so enticing: I could easily have bluffed my way through. But I knew it wasn't the best thing to do.

"And as I sit here today, I know it was my proudest moment of all: stepping down and letting somebody else take that position. That was me at my best. I knew that those behaviours that I was exhibiting was me at my best. I knew that my attitude was the right attitude and my mindset was composed of the right beliefs."

7.3 SCIENCE AND EVIDENCE

The concept of nature vs nurture has been repeatedly disproven through research and evidence. In fact, a great deal of psychology and neuroscientific research has shown that our beliefs can be upgraded. Science proves we can change!

For instance, the study of neuroplasticity describes our brain's ability to restructure itself by forming new neural pathways as we progress through life. We can use this ability to forge new connections in our brain to change our mindset and our belief system that in turn changes our behaviour. Hebb's Law (4) tells us that brain cells that fire together wire together. This means that neurons which are associated with a specific behaviour or action can function together and form a new neural pathway.

One example of this is the well-known London cab driver study (5) which showed that the longer someone had been driving a taxi, the larger their hippocampus became. The hippocampus is the part of the brain which stores visual-spatial memory. In the pre-GPS era, London cab drivers had to rely on their (expanding) brains to navigate London's tangle of streets.

The neuroscientist Dr Robert Cooper has suggested that there is both a hard-wired and a live-wired element to the human brain (6). The hard wires are your embedded habits and default mechanisms – in other words, what you could think of as your default human nature. The live wires represent your brain's ability to grow and change.

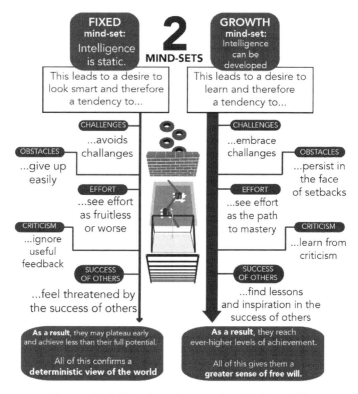

Figure 7.6 Fixed and growth mindsets (7)

Dr Cooper believes that these live wires can be up-wired and down-wired. Down-wiring means that we revert closer and closer to our default or 'hard wired' mode. Like hard-wiring, down-wiring can happen subconsciously over time. Up-wiring, on the other hand, is a conscious choice. When we choose to up-wire our brains, we are changing our mindset in a scientific manner.

Undertaking an exercise with this level of complexity may be difficult and challenging for many of us and requires a great deal of conscious effort. But it is nevertheless a very achievable and worthwhile process, and from the perspective of performance enhancement, it is essential. Vishen Lakhiani, founder and CEO of Mindvalley (8) and Carol Dweck, Professor of Psychology at Stanford University are both great proponents of this way of thinking, and the distinction between the 'fixed' and 'growth' mindsets, summarised in figure 7.6.

Dr Dweck said in a 2012 interview (9): "In a fixed mindset students believe their basic abilities, their intelligence, their talents, are just fixed traits. They have a certain amount and that's that, and then their goal becomes to look smart all the time and never look dumb. In a growth mindset students understand that their talents and abilities can be developed through effort, good teaching and persistence."

Lakhiani, Dweck and Cooper all believe that mindset is a flexible concept that can be retooled and re-educated - all you have to do is decide to make a change. And this is not a unique view – psychological interventions have been used for decades to increase skills and upscale performance.

Once we have identified the attitude that will carry us to our goal, we can choose specific thoughts to trigger the right hormones inside our body that will make us feel the way that we need to feel. It's all to do with how we frame the situation.

"If our beliefs are limited, they can drastically diminish our human potential. The problem is that our beliefs feel like reality because they are reality until you realise they are false." – Dave Asprey

Next, we can look at thought-induced brain chemistry and its effect on our physiological state. If we're in a stressed state for instance, we will release a lot of adrenalin and cortisol into our bloodstream. Conversely, happy thoughts deliver a release of hormones such as dehydroepiandrosterone (or DHEA), oxytocin and endorphins. Therefore, the hormones in our blood stream are representative of what we are thinking and feeling. So, it is easy to understand how our perception of the world and our perception of ourselves and how positive or negative we are feeling is very much in our blood.

When we are in a state of fear and we have cortisol and adrenalin flooding our system, our bodies focus on survival rather than growth. Inflammatory agents are released into our bloodstream and put us into a state of self-protection. Then, driven by our ancient survival mechanisms, not only does this state specifically prevent growth, it shuts down our immune systems as well in order to conserve energy for the fight or flight response. This is why states of fear are well connected to general poor health and long-term issues. This zero-growth, low immune system, high energy state is helpful if we're being chased by a lion, but not if we are trying to simply get ahead in life.

By becoming aware of our emotions and feelings, we can identify the root causes of our feelings and insert conscious thoughts followed by deliberate actions to change our experience of the world and be the person we want to be. Being able to do this means responding to our thoughts and questioning them, which can make the difference between a calm or chaotic life.

In the gaps between emotion, feeling, and acting, we all have the power to change and direct our lives for the better. Understanding our emotions and managing our feelings with conscious thinking is vital to prevent negative impulses from hijacking our brains. Science has taught us that we can actually change our brains through neuroplasticity, thought and behaviour. By taking control of this process, we can change our lives for the better.

In his book Atomic Habits (10), James Clear talks about the entrepreneur Jia Jiang, who set himself a challenge to seek out rejection for 100 days in a row. He believed that by doing this, he could hack his own fear, so that over time his body would stop going into a fear state when faced with rejection.

"To hack your own fear, Jia recommends celebrating failure," Clear writes. "When you play it safe, you won't be rejected. If you are willing to try something audacious enough that it fails, celebrate that. It is an accomplishment in and of itself."

One of the most effective forms of long-term behaviour change is the formation of habits. Through practice and repeated actions of a new behaviour or habit the connections of these neural pathways become established and strong, resulting in re-wiring in our brain.

Figure 7.7 shows there are three stages associated with successful habit formation which form a psychological pattern; the habit loop.

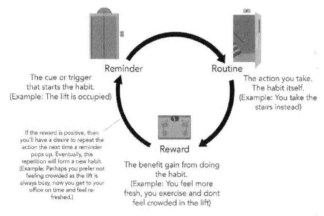

Figure 7.7 The 3 R's of Habit Formation (11)

Firstly, there is a cue or a trigger, that tells your brain to go into automatic mode and let a behaviour unfold – for instance, taking the same route home from work each day rather than choosing a different way. Secondly, there is the routine, which is the habit itself. Thirdly, there is a reward, something your brain likes that helps it recall the habit loop in the future.

Although it sounds straight-forward it is actually really difficult. Initially a lot of mental effort is required and dedication to repetition in order to create and imprint the neural pathway and therefore the habit loop. The pseudo-myth of a new behaviour or habit taking 21 days to form has been shown to be incorrect. Psychological research has now shown it takes an average of 66 days to form a new behaviour or habit. In addition, pathways that aren't used will weaken over time to allow room for new ones to form. This makes maintaining the habit difficult if it is not practised regularly. Therefore, warning signs indicating a breakdown in the desired new behaviour or habit need to be anticipated early and counteracted.

The good news is... everyone has the capacity for change and neuroplasticity isn't finite. The more we challenge and learn, the more adaptive our brains become.

So if we think about matching mindset, attitude and behaviour from a chemistry perspective, it is simply a construct from which we see the world, which elicits the flow of the corresponding hormones, positive or negative. Our attitude is the feelings that we experience, based on that hormonal release; and our behaviour is our physiological reaction driven by our sympathetic and parasympathetic nervous systems as response.

We can view this as a methodology to reduce the physiological effects of stress, by intentionally delivering more positive hormones into our systems to control the chemical composition of our blood.

Therefore a summary of how to address your response is detailed in figure 7.8.

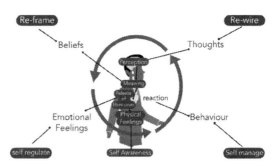

Figure 7.8 Rewiring your thoughts

REFERENCES

(1) Clear, J. (2018). Atomic Habits. Sevenoaks, UK: Cornerstone Digital. P.50.

(2) http://mveps.edublogs.org/files/2013/08/Betaris-Box-1up1a1y.pdf (Viewed July 2019).

(3) Walsh, V. 'A CBT look at anxious assessment versus calm assessment.' Veronica Walsh's CBT Blog. 2012. (cited July 2019). Available at: https://iveronicawalsh.wordpress.com/2013/06/02/a-cbt-look-at-anxious-assessment-versus-calm-assessment/

(4) Hebb, Donald.O. (1949). The organization of Behavior. New York: Wiley.

(5) Maguire, E.A., Woollett, K., Spiers H.J. (2006). London taxi drivers and bus drivers: a structural MRI and neuropsychological analysis. Wiley Online Library. Available at: https://onlinelibrary.wiley.com/doi/abs/10.1002/hipo.20233. (Viewed July 2019).

(6) Asprey, D. 'Robert Cooper: Rewiring Your Brain & Creating New Habits – #261'. Bulletproof Radio. 2015 (cited July 2019). Available at: https://blog.bulletproof.com/robert-cooper-rewiring-brain-creating-new-habits-261/

(7) Dweck, C. (2007). Mindset: The New Psychology of Success. New York: Ballantine.

(9) Lakhiani, V. (2016). The Code of the Extraordinary Mind. New York: Rodale.

(9) Morehead, J. 'Stanford University's Carol Dweck on the Growth Mindset and Education'. Onedublin.org [newspaper on the internet]. 2012 June 12. (cited July 2019). Available at: https://onedublin.org/2012/06/19/stanford-universitys-carol-dweck-on-the-growth-mindset-and-education/

(10) Clear, J. (2018). Atomic Habits. Sevenoaks, UK: Cornerstone Digital.

(11) Clear, J. 'Transform Your Habits: Learn How Psychology Makes It Easier for You to Live Healthily

and Actually Stick to Your Goals.' 2013. (Cited July 2019). Available at: https://jamesclear.com/wp-content/uploads/2013/09/habits-v2.pdf

7.4 HOW TO APPLY

To put what we have learned about taking control into action, take the time to consider your mindset, attitudes and behaviours when you are at your best and worst. The exercises will help you to understand what can be achieved.

A common self-limiting mindset we come up against in business, sport and general life is fear of failing. This belief is essentially "If I do that, there's a risk I'll fail, so I'm not going to try." Another that often goes hand in hand is a fear of making mistakes. This often has roots in childhood when we may have been led to believe that making mistakes is wrong and to be avoided.

Over time this becomes a subconscious belief, and our conscious thoughts that fundamentally reject this notion cannot overrule the more powerful subconscious belief created as children. Another big one is 'imposter syndrome': that sense that "I'm just not good enough to be able to do that. Who do I think I am?" which creates a limit to performance.

The first step to resolving these issues is reflection - to identify the self-limiting mindset that exists. Firstly, we need to recognise the internal story we tell ourselves, that we are not actually good enough. It is important to remove negative beliefs from our mindsets, so that we can develop an accurate source of feedback as we continue to develop our new positive mindset. This is especially important to avoid doubt creeping in and undermining our confidence.

Step 1 Identify the link between your mindset, attitudes and behaviours

Internal process	Coaching realisation points	Habit formation
Sense		Awareness
Perception	Thoughts	Rewire
Attribute meaning	Beliefs	Reframe
Release of hormones	Emotional feelings	Self regulate
	Physical feelings	Self awareness
Chosen behaviour	Behaviours	Self manage

Figure 7.9 internal, realisation and habit formation

We do not need to be prisoners to our body's natural chemistry. We all share similar internal processes – the gut reactions that we have in any given situation. But we can override any potentially damaging internal processes through habit formation. For instance, when we see our romantic partner, we are likely to experience a release of hormones and a flood of warm, affectionate feelings. But if we see our romantic partner sharing an intimate moment with another person, these feelings can quickly curdle into jealousy. However, by taking some time to understand our emotional feelings, we can train ourselves to regulate our reaction and avoid jumping to damaging conclusions.

The 'identify the link' exercise is designed to identify your current hardwired response to a situation, event or environment and to help you understand the link between your mindset, attitudes and behaviours. This will enable you to understand how you currently respond. Specificity and honesty is really important when it comes to improving and learning so pick one particular area you would like to improve and get a better outcome. Understanding how you currently respond enables you to think about how to change.

Exercise: Identify the link

The exercise encourages you to think honestly about how you respond to certain events. What are the worst and the best responses you could have in any particular situation?

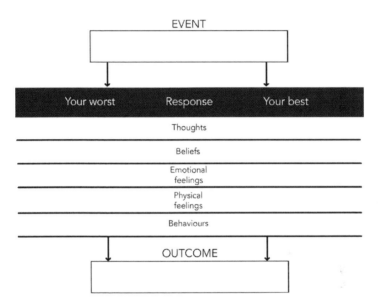

Even for the most resilient of us, reacting negatively to work situations where we perceive we are being criticised unfairly (even if we are not!) can have a negative outcome. With a deeper understanding of how your feelings, emotions, behaviours and outcomes are interlinked, how would you respond differently in a similar situation, whether at work, or perhaps at home or with family and friends?

And now to hack this hardwired response and get a better outcome! This time flip it and start with the outcome you want working up to the event. From these answers you will create your own approach to creating winning habits.

Exercise: The outcome you want to achieve

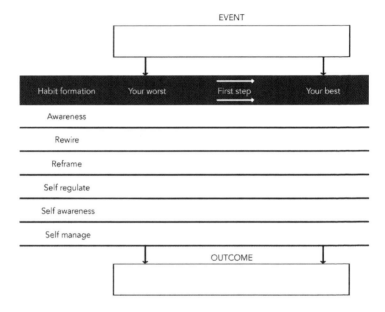

Step 2 – Habit formation
Emotional self-regulation - hack your system and make this a habit
Research has established that emotions are malleable. They can be changed by:

- Altering an external situation (for instance, by divorcing an abusive spouse)
- Shifting our attention (for instance, by choosing to focus on a more positive aspect of a situation)
- Re-appraising a situation (for instance, believing

that the upcoming test is an opportunity for learning, not an assessment of personal worth).

How we choose to live our lives has tremendous power over the way we feel every day.

Another important technique in applying these lessons is to upgrade our habits based on our upgraded beliefs. Our habits are really just the embodiment of our past behaviours, and we know that these behaviours can be changed. For most people, when talking about behaviour change or habit formation, the purpose is the outcome they are chasing, or the process itself. For instance they say "I want to get fit" (the outcome) or "I should go for a run" (the process). However, true behaviour change and effective habit formation comes from ingraining the goal as part of our identity and owning and living it as an identity change. So, the recommended statement becomes: "I am a runner" (identity). In this way we are integrating our beliefs into our identity.

It follows then, that the goal is not to learn a musical instrument, but to become a musician. Instead of "I want to stop smoking," you say "I don't smoke." or "I'm not a smoker".

It's important also to remember when setting up a habit that it's not about the length of time we work on it, it is the number of repetitions that counts. So, don't be tempted into the mindset that "if I do this for a month, I will form this habit" - it doesn't work that way. We need to keep reinforcing the pattern: that's what helps us to create new habits.

- How do we do this in sport, in business and in life?
- Declaration of intent - the athlete makes the desired habit or the behaviour change public in order to increase accountability and likelihood of commitment. This is particularly powerful in team or crew situations when the collective could support the individual for the common benefit.
- Determine the most effective reminder or cue for

the individual - for some athletes this could be a coaching prompt or a specific word, for others it is a visual cue or video feedback. The more powerful the cue the more frequently the routine will be carried out and the quicker the habit will form.

- Coach as our conscience - athletes use the team around them to hold them accountable and at times provide the reminder and/or reward.

Monitoring Progress

We can also use metrics to monitor our performance. This is easy in sport as we can video our performance for analysis. In business, we might want to analyse client reviews, colleague or team feedback or 360 review information. Habit tracking is another great way to assess progress - did you complete the habit each day? If not, why and how quickly did you get back on track? It's important that we consciously identify how we would like to be measured and where possible use a combination of qualitative and quantitative data on the actions and the reactions. So, we review our performance based on the objective rather than the subjective results. What did actually happen? What is the evidence? We can then use that data to look back through the process to identify what our feelings were at each stage, and identify the trigger points where we started to slip: how we actually felt at those moments, how had our attitude changed, and what was the behaviour the team observed?

Therefore, next time we do it, if we achieve the outcome and the beliefs were sound, what can we improve on next?

Then the question becomes: "What else can I be doing to help influence my performance in a positive way?" One way to stay on track is to use a buddy or team to monitor your behaviour. In this case it's important to be clear with the people that can help us with how we want to receive that feedback and how frequently.

But perhaps the best place to start is to develop a future aspiration: something challenging enough that you have to work at it consciously, but not so hard that it's impossible. Write your aspiration down on paper. The next step is to figure out what behaviours and habits are needed to make certain you can achieve that win. Again, write them down. Once you have those clearly outlined, begin figuring out what you must do to embody them. What will it take to set those habits up? Write down ways you can make them accessible and achievable.

Habit formation:

1. Decide who you want to be
2. Decide what mindset/attitude/feeling will get you there
3. Identify habits that will embody your chosen identity
4. Prove it to yourself with small wins

Download the workbook for this chapter at: *WhatDoesItTakeToWin.com/workbook*

7.6 SUMMARY

Taking control so we can be at our best is a choice that anyone can make. Making this choice is the first step in a scientifically proven process by which we can learn to break bad habits and rewire our brains to make better decisions. In this chapter, we have seen how this whole process begins with a moment of realisation - an experience which can be somewhat painful, as David learned when he realised how his turns were holding him back.

"In this section we have talked about using attitude and mindset to elicit the optimal behaviour, so we can command that control which allows us to choose to perform at our best. And I look back and compare it to the experiences I had in 2004 and 2008.

"In Athens 2004 a decision had gone against me and I had gone off in a huff. I closed myself off, refused to reach out. I was judging one group and blaming another. I had so many negative thoughts running around my head reinforcing the anger and frustration inside me. And I felt strongly justified to be angry and to believe those negative thoughts. I had a similar experience in 2008 when I missed the gold by 0.8 seconds. It took me four years to get out of that dark place of thinking."

This is the point at which we start to take ownership of our true identity, disconnect from our old belief systems and replace our self-limiting beliefs with a flexible mindset that asks the right questions and challenges our false assumptions. And it all begins with the mindset. Our mindset is composed of thoughts and beliefs that stimulate the release of corresponding hormones which flow around our bodies. These hormones largely determine our experience of life and govern our attitude and behaviour.

This is where we turn to science. Hebb's Rule proves that our brain cells can be trained to work together to form a new neural pathway – this means that we can effectively 'rewire' our brains to change the way we react and respond in a stressful or competitive situation.

Behaviour is the easiest element to control and important if we want to lead and prove ourselves authentic. The Betaris Concept shows us the influence that our behaviour has on others, and how their reactions feed back to us and influence us in return. But changing behaviour is not as simple as it sounds. We must change the belief underlying our behaviour first and then practise consistency in our new habits. We can do this by actively challenging our beliefs and intimately examining their origins.

It can help to remember that our feelings are not correlated with reality: feelings are purely the result of the thoughts we allow to pass through our minds, and as Gandhi said, positive thoughts are the first step on the way towards positive behaviour. It is as simple as that.

To visualise this process in real life, it can be helpful to identify a challenging but achievable goal and understand what fears might be standing in our way. We must also determine what accessible and achievable habits and behaviours are needed to make certain we can achieve that goal. Next, we determine the mindset we need to adopt that will result in those habits and behaviours. And finally, we begin to adopt the new habits and continually re-evaluate in a positive habit loop.

Scientific research and psychological analysis has repeatedly shown that our beliefs can be upgraded, if we choose to make a change. If we refine our mindset, we can redefine our attitude, redevelop our beliefs and create positive behavioural patterns that match our goals. From a chemistry perspective, the objective is to manage our thoughts and emotions to intentionally trigger the release of preferable hormonal blends into our systems to control the chemical composition of our blood. In doing this, we can boost our cognitive and immune functions, enhance our alertness and increase our attention.

Achieving big goals is not meant to be easy. Failure is an ever-present safety net that can sometimes hold us back from achieving our full potential. We need a resilient mental attitude to endure the failures we are certain to experience while we edge closer and closer to our goal, and to maintain our motivation and keep going.

David knows this better than most people. During his training for London 2012, he realised that his slow turns were holding him back – a realisation that led to action, and a new, more effective habit loop. And then, in the height of Olympic fever, David experienced the surprising culmination of his training. After giving everything in the pool, he demonstrated his ability to silence his ambition and put his team before himself by manifesting those behaviours that represented his very best. Because his mindset and attitude were in complete alignment with his purpose, David established total control of how he was behaving and how he felt. He had chosen to be at his best and in realising his best he achieved the highest level of fulfilment.

"Regardless of the environment that we find ourselves in, to perform at our absolute best, we need to be in control of our thoughts and our attitude. Once you have identified the attitude that will carry you to your goal, you can choose specific thoughts to trigger the right hormones inside your body that will make you feel the way that you need to feel. It's all to do with how you frame the situation. The feeling that I had of being totally fine with not swimming in that final was a huge, huge feeling for me, completely different to any other feelings I'd ever had. To not only personally perform at my best but then perform at my best as a team player brought the realisation that I was utterly in control of how I behaved and utterly in control of how I feel. I was in control of my mindset. And I had chosen to be at my best."

Chapter 8

Learn to learn
– Review to be better

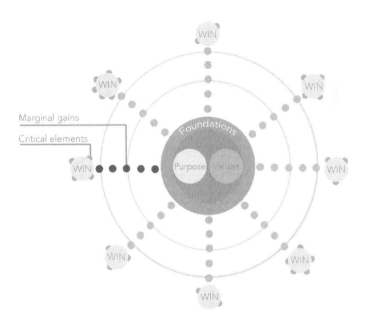

8.1 INTRODUCING PLANNING TO LEARN

Learning never stops. We must keep reinforcing our good habits through practice and performance to give ourselves the best possible chance of reaching this win and all future wins.

We have now reached the outer edges of our atom – we have achieved our win, or we are in the process of achieving it. We now have all the tools that we need to build our success, now our challenge is to apply them. The more we utilise them, the more skilled we will become, and we can use these skills to be the best version of ourselves in our everyday life. We do this by following a simple cycle of learning, as shown in figure 8.1

The Action Learning Cycle

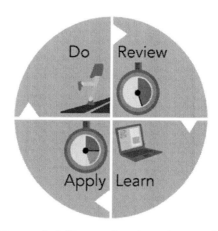

Figure 8.1 The action learning cycle

In this chapter, we will come across a variety of different learning cycles, each one emphasising a different type of behaviour or attitude. But they all have one thing in common, they are all cyclical. Learning is an iterative and ongoing process. It does not begin and end at a fixed point – it allows the space for one lesson to roll into the next.

This is a particularly important thing to consider when we are trying to learn from a win – regardless of whether or not that win has actually been achieved.

David Carry experienced this at the 2008 Beijing Olympics, when he analysed his relay performance with the help of an expert coach. The relay is made up of four 200m stages, and David swam the final 200m, missing out on a medal by just a fraction of a second.

His coach broke down his performance into four 50m sections and analysed each one to get a sense of his pacing, when compared to the pacing of other world champions and Olympic swimmers.

"We found that I was about the seventh quickest in the 200m freestyle race, and I felt very satisfied with that performance," remembers David.

"Then the coach said that based on his analysis, for 75% of the race, I was the second fastest swimmer in the world – only Michael Phelps was quicker than me when I was swimming.

"Of course, I was delighted with this. But then he told me about the other 25%. When it came to my turns and starts, I wasn't even ranking in the top 100. This was having a huge effect on my overall performance.

"Initially, I was incredibly embarrassed. I went into a bit of a huff around this idea that I was terrible at my performance. But the amazing thing was that after I cooled off a little, I suddenly realised – hang on – all I have to do is to become average at that 25% and maintain my ability to swim as quickly as I was, and my performance was going to dramatically increase. That experience really triggered this new approach.

"In that moment I realised that I'm not the final package and life is about constantly trying to find out new and different ways to improve and develop and get better. This is just as true in sports as it is in business and in life."

The path to every end win will provide some valuable lessons that we can apply to our next win and the win after that. When we give ourselves time to reflect and review, our successes and failures become clearer and we can see what we need to repeat and what we need to avoid the next time around. If the win did not happen as planned, perhaps our first error occurred in the value-setting phase, when we overlooked or misrepresented a key value which made it more difficult to achieve the win. Or maybe our issues took root when we were portioning out our energy and prioritised incorrectly. Or perhaps we simply missed out a marginal gain which would have helped us to fulfil one of our critical elements, leaving us underprepared for the win.

Of course, we can also look back from the vantage point of a more successful win and see we more or less made all the right choices. This is one of the benefits of hindsight, our journey to the outcome will always be coloured by the conclusion itself. We achieve our win and we imagine that we must be something special. We fail to achieve it and we look back on our journey with a negative bias, seeing nothing but flaws.

On every journey to every win there will be things that we have done right and things that we have done wrong. In order to learn, we need to look at everything – the good and the bad – and apply the same reasoning to both. There will always be a lesson to learn. When we have extracted all of our learning from our journey and outcome, we can apply it to our next journey and the cycle repeats, but it gets incrementally better each time.

8.2 DEFINING

When we learn to learn, we are gifting ourselves with the ability to keep on growing and exceeding our own ambitions. A devotion to learning is rewarded with knowledge, experience, and – yes – confidence. But how do we learn to learn?

There are many learning models that we can refer to when we decide to focus on our learning skills. Kolb's Learning Cycle, for instance, emphasises the importance of reflecting on our experiences, extracting some key learning points, and then experimenting with new actions, before repeating the cycle all over again. We do this until we know what works and what doesn't work for us and our ability to reach our win. Then we do it again until we have finessed the process.

Learning is a cycle and reviewing performance is a key step in completing that cycle. Many of us find it difficult to take time to pause and allow space for self-reflection. This does not mean simply observing the outcome and reflecting on it – true reflection requires us to go deeper than that and think about our own behaviours and beliefs.

How to reflect

We define self reflection as: careful thought about our own behaviour and beliefs. We can also give careful thought to an experience, a change we have undergone or a learning event.

When we reflect, we must begin by thinking about what we intended to do. What was the critical element? And how did we set out to pursue that element? What was the intention? What was the reality? This goes far beyond just looking at the outcome – it is about breaking down the whole process and working out what went right and what went wrong. This is also an opportunity for us to review the knowns and the unknowns. How did we manage to overcome the problems that we had predicted? And what unknowns did we discover along the way? One of the great benefits of reflection is that it turns those unknowns into knowns, so we are better able to predict and handle them the next time around.

At the London 2012 Olympics, Hannah MacLeod's field

hockey team set out with the intention to win gold. The reality was that they won the bronze medal.

"When we came away with bronze at London 2012, it was seen as a failure, internally and externally, even though it was the first Olympic medal we'd won in 20 years," she recalls.

"We probably weren't even the third best team there, but we really benefitted from a home Olympics and a few other results going our way. We probably exceeded our potential and bronze was a massive success. With what we achieved with that group of players, I can honestly look back at those three years and go, 'We could not have done any more.' It was a really tough three years. So how on earth can that be failure?"

Two years later, the team came eleventh out of twelve teams at the World Cup. But after a period of reflection, they went on to achieve their intention of winning gold at Rio 2016.

Hannah explains how this happened.

"We reviewed our performance at London 2012, but we only focused on all the things we could have done better," she says. "So we went about our changes without ever consolidating all the things that we had done so well to move us from a world ranking of 7th in the world to our first Olympic medal in 20 years."

"Two years later we came eleventh out of twelve at the World Cup. There were massive expectations - for the sake of our funding we needed to win a medal and it was an absolute horror show. But there were many signs that that performance was going to happen and sure enough, there it was. It was the lowest point, probably, of my life and my career. I very nearly walked away from the sport because I didn't understand or believe in what we were doing.

"Eighteen months later we won Olympic gold at Rio. What it boiled down to was the opportunity for the team to speak openly and honestly and reflect on all the good things that had gone before.

"There were no magic bullets – just tiny behaviours that drove high-performance. It was, 'Does everyone really understand their role?' 'What's our level of trust and respect amongst the team?' People were not wearing the right kit, they were turning up late for meetings and you start to second-guess why they're late, 'Well it's because they don't respect me.' So that starts to snowball. And all these small behaviours really add up within a performance environment where there is a lot of stress, a lot of pressure. And it culminated in our performances on the pitch falling away, dramatically.

"We spent two days in facilitated discussions, and in a very short space of time, our culture started to shift. And it came down to a focus on behaviour and permission to challenge and hold each other accountable. It was the same people, absolutely the same people, but once you challenge the cultural norms, you invest in understanding what your purpose is, what your values are, and then ultimately you discuss the behaviours that need to be seen on a day-to-day basis. If you're given time to discuss that and there's a degree of ownership over it, you can then hold each other accountable. That was fundamental in reshaping the direction of that group of individuals."

By reflecting honestly on their performance and their team mindset, the hockey team was able to almost instantly change their performance.

There are three clear benefits of self reflection:

1. Strengthening emotional intelligence

When taking time to self-reflect, we are giving ourselves permission to look inwards. This helps to build two key components to emotional intelligence: self-awareness and self-regulation. Self-awareness gives us the ability to understand our emotions, strengths, weaknesses, drives, values and goals, and recognise its impact on others. Self-regulation involves the ability to control or redirect our disruptive emotions and impulses and adapt to changing circumstances. These skills can be useful in both our personal lives and our professional lives.

2. Acting with integrity

Becoming clear on our core values will help to strengthen our integrity and lead us to better decisions. Our integrity is often put to the test during stressful times. Taking time to review our key decisions and actions in the recent past and evaluating them against our core values is critical to acting with integrity. Doing this consistently can solidify our values and make the decision-making process easier in the future.

3. Being more confident

Confidence is crucial for managing a busy, complex life that includes meeting career, family, community and personal needs. It helps in effective communications, decision-making, and influence building. The more we reflect on our strengths and how we can build upon them, the more confident we will be in the future.

Many people fall into the trap of simply reviewing the outcome and assuming that their review is enough, and they have learned from their mistakes. But reflecting and reviewing are two different things. When we reflect, we explore all the interactions that have happened along the way - the behaviours, the mindsets and the critical elements. This is how we understand where and how something has gone wrong, and what tiny thing could have been done differently to achieve a different outcome. Each time we reflect, we should be getting closer to living our true identity and values.

"If I as an athlete discovered something that I was really bad at, it was such a moment of celebration because it gave me a better chance of being successful," says David Carry. "And being able to have that dispassionate, almost disconnected view of what I had done in relation to what I want to do, was so important it was almost with a childlike wonderment that I was able to look at my own performance and go, 'Wow, that was really bad.

Hah, who knew? I didn't even see that coming'. And now that I've got this fresh information with a view to where I want to try and get to, that is going to be a massive opportunity for me to get closer to that."

Feedback

Getting feedback is a brilliant way to accelerate our learning, but only if we approach it in the right manner. Often when we seek out feedback, what we are really doing is looking for reinforcement and praise. This may feel good in the moment, but we are never going to improve if we are constantly being told that we are doing great. Everyone is guilty of this – even Olympic athletes.

"When I was younger, I would go to somebody who I knew full well would only tell me the story I want to hear, so whether it's a coach, whether it's a key stake-holder, however you want to term it," explains Hannah. "I would go to that individual with the loose intention of getting feedback but all I really wanted to hear was them tell me that I'm wonderful. So, my behaviour was that of somebody who was seeking feedback, but the reality was that I was only prepared to listen to one story.

"In that moment, I genuinely believed I was after feedback. I would almost subconsciously go to people who I knew wouldn't hurt me because I wasn't strong enough, confident enough, didn't have the foundations in place to listen to messages that would absolutely floor me. So, if anyone picked anything apart or actually offered some objective, helpful advice that would promote my learning or help develop my learning, I was not prepared to listen to it."

This feedback loop happens all the time in corporate environments, particularly in upper management. There are a lot of C-suite executives who are surrounded by yes people – either by design or as a result of the working environment that they have created. They may be actively seeking feedback on a daily basis, but all they are ever going to hear is that their decisions are right.

This is a comfortable place to be, so unless the executive is particularly insightful and committed to growth, the feedback loop is likely to continue. The side effect of this is that the company never develops, and talented employees are not recognised.

To break this cycle, there must be a genuine desire to challenge the view of the world that they have, and to seek out the blind spots in their leadership.

Hindsight bias

Hindsight bias happens when we take a skewed view of the past, based on a bad outcome. For instance, say our win is to complete a triathlon, but we get a bad cramp during the swimming stage and have to bow out. It would be easy to fall into a negative thought pattern, telling ourselves that we have failed, that we didn't plan properly, that we've let ourselves down.

When alongside a negative mindset, hindsight bias can be counterproductive to our learning. By allowing self-doubt to creep in at this stage, we will find ourselves thinking things like "I should have done this," or, "I could have done that". This is not helpful for the learning process. Instead, we need to take a more analytical approach. We need to look at the causes behind a disappointing outcome – did we have the right beliefs, behaviours, attitude, and mindset? Did we remain focused on our fundamentals while we were chasing our win? Perhaps we overlooked one of our marginal gains somewhere along the way, putting us at higher risk of cramping. Did we follow the correct diet? Did we stretch properly before the race? Once we start asking productive questions, we can work out what we will do differently next time rather than associating blame or attributing failure to external circumstances.

However, we must be aware that if we know that an outcome is really bad, this will influence how we see the behaviour leading up to it. We will be more likely to look for mistakes, or even negligence. We will be less inclined to see the behaviour as forgivable. The worse the outcome is, the more likely we are to see mistakes.

Hindsight means that we are at risk of oversimplifying causality because we are starting from the outcome and working backwards to find presumed or possible causes. We overestimate the likelihood of the outcome because we already have the outcome in our hands: 'It's no wonder I got a cramp while I was swimming – I left my banana in the car.' We can misjudge the prominence or relevance of the moments leading up to the outcome, in the search for a quick and easy explanation for our performance. If the outcome was bad, we think, then the actions must have been bad too.

Overcoming hindsight bias is very hard, but it is not impossible. The theory of 'systems thinking' explained in table suggests the behaviour of a system's components can only be understood by examining the context in which that behaviour occurs. Viewing behaviour in isolation from the surrounding system prevents full understanding of why failure occurred — and thus the opportunity to learn from it.

The Five Values of Systems Thinking

THE FIVE VALUES OF SYSTEMS THINKING	
Transparency	= communicating thoughts and actions to others.
Integrity	= giving and receiving feedback without being defensive.
Issue orientation	= focusing on the relevance of information to the issues at hand, regardless of extraneous factors such as hidden agendas.
Inquiry	= persisting until a satisfactory understanding is achieved.
Accountability	= assuming responsibility for learning and the implementation of lessons learned.

In order to think systemically rather than emotionally, we need follow the five values listed above: transparency, integrity, issue orientation, inquiry and accountability.

In 'systems thinking', human error is considered to be a symptom, not a cause. All human behaviour is affected by the context in which it occurs. To understand and do something about such error, we must look at the system in which people work, for example; the design of the equipment, the usefulness of procedures, and the existence of goal conflicts and production pressures. In fact, we could even claim that human error is a symptom of a system that needs to be redesigned. However, if we try to change the person rather than the system itself, we are doomed to failure.

The first step in applying systemic thinking is to assume that nobody comes to work with the intention of doing a bad job. The person explaining what happened and why it happened needs to assume that the people involved were doing reasonable things, or at least what they thought was reasonable, given the complexities, dilemmas, trade-offs and uncertainty surrounding the events. Simply highlighting their mistakes provides no useful information for preventing future accidents.

Remember, we are not reflecting for the sake of reflection – we are trying to learn from our past actions. If we are not able find the lesson in our outcome, we have clearly missed something important along the way.

Things do not go well because people simply follow the procedures and work as imagined. Things go well because people make sensible adjustments according to the demands of the situation.

Finding out what these adjustments are and trying to learn from them is at least as important as finding the causes of adverse outcomes.

8.3 SCIENCE AND EVIDENCE

"There are two goals in the experiential learning process. One is to learn the specifics of a particular subject, and the other is to learn about one's own learning process." – David Kolb

Active learning does not involve memorising long texts and quoting scholars. Real learning happens when we can re-live our past experiences without making the same mistakes again and repeat the lessons that have been proven to work.

We have already performed a pre-mortem on our win, and now that we have put our plans into action, we can perform the post-mortem.

Perhaps the best-known example of this approach is the U.S. Army's After Action Review (AAR) process (2), which is now widely used by many organisations in staff training. It involves a systematic debriefing after every mission, project, or critical activity. This process is framed by four simple questions:

(1) What did we set out to do?
(2) What actually happened?
(3) Why did it happen?
(4) What do we do next time?

For the AAR process to be successful, the team needs to discover for itself the lessons provided by the experience. The more open and honest the discussion, the better.

One of the original authors of AAR, Charles S. Parry, revisited the process a few years later, adapting it specifically for business use and calling it the After Review Cycle (ARC) (3).

Two categories of action lend themselves to an ARC, he explains. First: activities that are repeated regularly but not often, such as quarterly presentations to investors.

"In between those presentations are three months during which people get fuzzy about what worked, what didn't, and where they thought they could do better," Parry says. "Learning from our mistakes sounds good. But unless you're learning from the past in service to the future, it's not that important.

"You don't want to do an inquest. You want people leaning forward."

All learning begins with willingness on the part of individual to learn from every experience, to develop a culture of self-monitoring and self-reflection in order to draw out the lessons learned and to act upon them in the future.

This means that the debrief process becomes a critical developmental step on the road to excellence, and this takes on greater significance following unsuccessful performances compared to successful ones.

In sport, these debriefs usually focus on the behaviours, thoughts and emotional responses that proved productive as well as those that proved unproductive. The aim of the process is not to dwell on the mistakes made, but rather to crystallise the lessons learned from those mistakes for future reference. This is an important step in regaining a sense of control following a failure in sport – and it is a process which David Carry and Hannah McLeod have both learned through first-hand experience.

Ongoing learning through self-reflection is time consuming and it can be an unpleasant experience to dissect a poor performance. Ultimately, however, it is a timesaver. If we do not learn from our mistakes, we are destined to repeat them.

"Ideas are not fixed elements of thought, but are formed and re-formed through experience"
- *David A. Kolb*

David Kolb was one of the first people to develop the experiential learning theory (ELT) (5). This is a dynamic theory based on a learning cycle which is driven by two main behaviours: action/reflection and experience/abstraction.

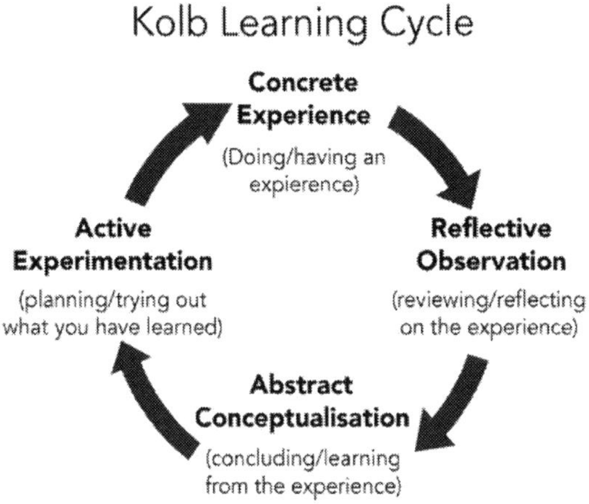

Kolb Learning Cycle

Figure 8.2 The Kolb Learning Cycle (1)

The ELT model is made up of four stages: concrete experience, reflective observation, abstract conceptualisation, and active experimentation as depicted in figure 8.2. There is no definitive starting point or end point – the purpose of the model is to encourage analysis and repetition.

There are many other iterations of learning theory. Transformative learning is the process of "perspective transformation", with three dimensions: behavioural (changes in lifestyle), psychological (changes in understanding of the self), and convictional (revision of belief systems).

Endless studies have attempted to find a common thread that will explain once and for all how we learn and retain information, but ultimately it all comes down to one thing: practice.

Repetition and reinforcement are two of the most effective strategies when we are learning to learn. Whether we are conducting our post-mortem, applying our journey to the Kolb Learning Cycle, or experimenting with different ways of learning – by committing to do, learn and repeat, we will ensure our ongoing growth, no matter what our win may be.

REFERENCES

(1) Kolb, D. A., Kolb, Alice Y. (2011). The Kolb Learning Style Inventory: A Comprehensive Guide to the Theory, Psychometrics, Research on Validity and Educational Applications. Experiential learning: Experience as the source of learning and development (Version 4.0). Experience Based Learning Systems. Available at: https://learningfromexperience.com/downloads/research-library/the-kolb-learning-style-inventory-4-0.pdf). [viewed June 2019]. P.8

(2) Parry, Charles S. and Darling, Marilyn J. (2001) Emergent Learning in Action: The After Action Review. The Systems Thinker no. 12 vol. 8

(3) Parry, Charles S. and DeGrosky, Michael T. (2011) Beyond the AAR: The Action Review Cycle (ARC). Proceedings of 11th International Wildland Fire Safety Summit, Missoula, Montana, USA. Available at https://www.researchgate.net/publication/228452347_Beyond_the_AAR_The_Action_Review_Cycle_ARC [viewed June 2019].

(4) Kolb, D. A. (1984). Experiential learning: Experience as the source of learning and development (Vol. 1). Englewood Cliffs, NJ: Prentice-Hall. P.85

(5) Kolb, D. A. (1984). Experiential learning: Experience as the source of learning and development (Vol. 1). Englewood Cliffs, NJ: Prentice-Hall.

8.4 HOW TO APPLY

In order to learn from our experiences, we need to ask ourselves a few key questions.

These questions are roughly in line with the various models for learning that we just discussed. In order to learn, we need information – good and bad. We then need to apply that information to our journey in order to make a change.

What was the intention?

First, we need to ask ourselves what did we set out to do? What was the win that we had in mind when we began this process? For instance, if our win was to overcome a fear of heights and complete a skydive, has that opportunity presented itself yet? Have we created the opportunity for ourselves?

Was it achieved?

This may seem like an easy question to answer, but it requires some thought. If you have completed the skydive, then that's great – job done! If not, there may be another indicator of progress that we are missing. Did you make it into the airplane? This could be seen as a mini win or a marginal gain for someone who has a terrible phobia of flying. However, it may not mean that the win was achieved.

What happened?

This is the point where we have to interrogate our process. It may be helpful to go back through this book from the start and look for gaps in our understanding or actions. Do we understand the difference between the purpose and the win? Was the win attainable? Has our concept of the win changed over time? Did we meet all of our critical elements? For example, if one of the critical elements behind the skydive was raising money for charity, did we accomplish this? And if not, why? Perhaps we were not as committed to the idea as we thought we were and allowed other elements to take priority.

What will we do differently?

As we know, it is always easier to see the negatives in hindsight, so this question should be easy to answer. However, it will not be helpful to put ourselves down by listing variations on 'I'm not good enough'. We need to look at the points where we veered off track and isolate each one of these moments until we understand where, how and why it went wrong. Then we need to filter these moments through the Kolb Learning Cycle until we have eliminated the errors from our process.

What will we replicate?

It is extremely unlikely that we did everything wrong. However, when we are dissatisfied with the outcome of our win, it can be hard to see the positives. Maybe we failed to do the skydive, but we did manage to stand at the edge of the airplane and look down without fainting in fear! Rather than focusing on the negatives, we need to take a moment to acknowledge the things that went well, and then ensure that we replicate them next time.

Reinforcing good behaviours is just as important as eliminating bad ones. Ask yourself, what are your super strengths? We all have a few things that we do better than most, and we can lean on those strengths as we continue to learn. These super strengths are usually linked with our values, so by focusing on these strengths we should be able to move closer to our win.

Exercise: Key questions to help us learn

What was the intention?	
Was it achieved?	
What happened? (what went wrong/right – why?)	
What will we do differently next time?	
What can we replicate?	

One final question...

There is one more question that we must ask ourselves to ensure that we are committed to this learning process: What habits do we currently have in place to ensure active learning?

Our learning never stops. We can always do things differently and more efficiently. It would be easy to just relax once we have achieved our end win, but why would we do that when we now know how much we are capable of? This journey has equipped us with the tools we need to overcome our fears, identify our values, set our purpose, and maximise our chances of success by eliminating the things that drag us back, and prioritising the things that propel us forward.

With these skills at our disposal, there is nothing we can't do. Use this win as the template for future successes and keep on growing and learning.

Exercise: The habits

Habit	How does this ensure active learning?

Download the workbook for this chapter at: *WhatDoesIt-TakeToWin.com/workbook*

8.5 SUMMARY AND CONCLUSION

Learning is challenging, it requires time and it requires a certain level of honesty that not everyone is ready for. It can be hard to acknowledge our own shortcomings, especially when we have worked so hard and done so many things right. But this is all a part of the learning experience as well – as much as we want to avoid making the same mistakes twice, we also want to repeat our successes again and again.

The most positive form of learning happens when we reframe our shortcomings as opportunities to improve and become the best versions of ourselves. This may involve revisiting the earlier chapters of this book and taking another look at our values, our mindset and our behaviour, as well as our critical elements and our marginal gains.

There is no end point to learning. We all have the capacity within ourselves, with the correct mindset, to continue to develop as humans. But we must have that willingness to learn and to grow. This means building an ability to see our flaws as well as our talents – to see where we need to put in a bit more work, and to celebrate the opportunity to keep on learning.

When we know where we need to improve, we can place our focus there and make sure we don't make the same mistakes twice. Likewise, by reflecting on our successes, we can replicate them in other areas of our lives. When we know what we do well and how to maximise the benefits, our confidence will grow and grow.

Now that you have read this book, you can apply all of your learning to any area of your life where you want to see a change. This same process can be used in sports, in business and in life itself, to help us to reach our full potential and gain confidence through our successes and our ability to live according to our values.

There is no end to what we can achieve if we approach our wins with the spirit of an Olympian and the mindset of a psychologist. By living the eight choices in this book, you can achieve more than you previously thought possible. And once you've done that, you can start setting ever-more ambitious targets for the future.

What will your next win be?

Printed by Amazon Italia Logistica S.r.l.
Torrazza Piemonte (TO), Italy

10276836R00116